ON CRICKET

ALSO BY SIR TREVOR McDONALD

An Improbable Life: The Autobiography

SIR TREVOR McDONALD

ON CRICKET

RENE
GADE

RENEGADE BOOKS

First published in Great Britain in 2024 by Renegade Books

1 3 5 7 9 10 8 6 4 2

A CIP catalogue record for this book
is available from the British Library.

Hardback ISBN 978-0-349-70506-4

Typeset in Berling by M Rules
Printed and bound in Great Britain by
Clays Ltd, Elcograf S.p.A

Papers used by Renegade Books are from well-managed forests
and other responsible sources.

Renegade Books
An imprint of Dialogue
Carmelite House
50 Victoria Embankment
London EC4Y 0DZ

www.dialoguebooks.co.uk

Dialogue, part of Little, Brown Book Group Limited,
an Hachette UK company.

CONTENTS

To the most wonderful parents in the world whose loving guidance equipped me with all the tools needed to survive. To the family whose unfailing love sustained me at every turn. And to the countless friends and colleagues without whose help, given so willingly, I would never have made it.

Play Up

This they all with a joyful mind
Bear through life like a torch in flame,
And falling fling to the host behind –
'Play up! play up! and play the game!'

'Vitaï Lampada',
SIR HENRY NEWBOLT

During the period of my life when my job required me to travel the world, whenever I arrived at a place, especially if it was dangerous, I would make sure to call my mother and tell her I was well, or, at least, alive. Her most frequent response when I told her I was in Moscow, or Beirut or Belfast was, 'But why?' A fair question and one I often found it dispiritingly difficult to give a simple answer to.

One particular time, I remember calling her from Beirut in Lebanon. At this point, in 1983, it was arguably one of the most dangerous places on earth. The previous year the city had been under siege after the breakdown of the UN-imposed ceasefire with Israel. There were to be deadly bombings and the PLO were about to be expelled. I felt that queasy mix of professional pride and personal anxiety that accompanied so much of my work as a foreign correspondent.

I greeted my mother, told her where I was, and began to reassure her I was safe when, without missing a beat, she began, 'How could the West Indies do that?' I knew immediately of course that she was referring to the West Indian loss to India in the final of the Cricket World Cup. My mother, like many women from the Caribbean, treated cricket like English people treat the weather: that is, an unavoidable and essential feature of daily life that must be dealt with first before subjects of secondary importance can be broached. As a son of those islands, I felt exactly the same way. And I suppose if this story has a centre it is one simple question: why?

I have written one previous book about myself. It was an attempt, at least, to capture the full shape of a life; a canvas in which I remained far more interested in those I had met than myself. Perhaps because that has been written, I want this to be a different sort of book. I think of it more as a series of intimate studies of my life's abiding passion. Cricket was my first obsession. In many ways it has remained my most consistent one. And, like all obsessions, it touches upon every other area of my life.

It was with me in those sprawling, never-ending games played with tree branches and tennis balls dipped in water, on dusty tarmac and any waste ground we could lay claim to, in our village in San Fernando, Trinidad, when my younger brother and I would be called back as the light failed. It was with me when I wanted to listen to cricket matches, so much so that my father eventually bought a radio. And it was through this battered box that I first listened to the BBC World Service. It was when listening to the ways that words created those faraway games, as I tested the shape of those distant cities in my mouth, that I first started to wonder if I might ever see them. It was with me when I began a school radio station and read news and cricket bulletins to my bemused schoolmates in secondary school. It was with me when I joined Radio Trinidad and, unable to persuade them I was a cricket commentator, tricked my way to Grenada to commentate on a cricket game. It was with me when I joined the BBC Bush House cricket team upon arrival in London in 1969, desperate for things that felt like home. It was with me in 1973, as a cub ITN reporter, when we played careful shots on the rooftops of the Ulster Television Studios at the height of the Troubles. It was with me when I travelled to South Africa to report on the evil apartheid system. It was with me when Saddam Hussein played every one of my deliveries with the straightest of bats. It was with me when I explained to an increasingly baffled and then irate US ambassador that, yes, we stopped for tea and lunch, matches lasted for five days and, at the end, it very well may be a draw. ('Well, that just sums the entire country up.') The comedian Robin Williams, of course, once memorably described cricket as 'baseball on Valium'. My sister still can't quite understand how I turned down the chance to attend a party at Brian Lara's house because I had to go back to my hotel room and prepare for an interview the next day. It is rumoured that each of his rooms is named after an English bowler he hit for a century.

It can sometimes feel as if the rest of my life was what happened when cricket wasn't happening. There is a single ground in Richmond where more than thirty years ago I once made 50 runs. Whenever I have passed it, I take a moment to savour this memory. Would I say it was my finest moment? Almost certainly.

Cricket has been with me through all of the vicissitudes and vagaries of my life. I cannot imagine my life without it. Like for many other fans, cricket has often felt more than a sport: rather, some essential element of my character. A desire to play life with a straight bat, however sticky the wicket. We were all taught that this was the way to be. To celebrate fair play, to respect the rules. Anything else just wasn't cricket. People are passionate about other sports. The love for football in England is immense. But you wouldn't ever hear someone say something 'wasn't football' in quite the same way. There is no pretence that you can use it as a metaphor for life.

To someone who has always so admired those batsmen who walk before they are called, there is something especially debased about much of contemporary public life. Today, certainly where politics is concerned, we live in a shameless era, when even if the umpire calls you out, you don't walk. You accuse the umpire of bias, you deny there was ever a ball, perhaps you accuse cricket itself of being in thrall to some shadowy elite. You deny that you are wearing cricket whites, that you have ever held a bat; indeed, that you even know what a bat is. Even if you are finally forced to walk, you hide in the clubhouse and hope everyone forgets and you can come back out to bat. Perhaps this time as captain.

To me growing up, the values of cricket were how you tried to live your life. My mother and father took the British Empire at its word. That if you worked hard, always tried your best, then you had an equal chance of success as any other subject. I am not so naive to believe that this was the case, but it is equally hard to look back in only anger, because it is my mother's face I see when I think of those ideas, and it is my father's voice I hear. I grew up, a boy, reading Shelley, Tennyson and Browning, T. S. Eliot and Shakespeare. And as I have grown older, I certainly have reflected upon how this might have shaped my generation's ability to see itself, to imagine what, as an individual, one is capable of. It is perhaps the dominant view now to see that inculcation of only British authors to a young Trinidadian boy as a wholly negative thing. And I can see that. Who can say what would have happened if V. S. Naipaul, C. L. R. James or Derek Walcott had been born fifty years earlier? If their words had been part of what I'd encountered as that young child? Had those words been presented to me as being of value? But do I regret encountering those glimmering words I did? No. I cannot. As with many people's relationship with their mother, a relationship with a mother country can be complicated.

The interrelation of cricket and colonialism is far too big a subject for me to do justice to. All I know is that nowhere outside of the Caribbean have I encountered quite the same flavour of obsession. Cricket pollinated throughout the world and produced different flowers in different soils. The Indians and Pakistanis adore cricket, of course. The English are the keepers of its holy book of *Wisden* (and by extension, they are sure, its soul); the Australians embrace it as a space in which to manifest their iron will to win; the South Africans don't need to be told about cricket as an engine of national identity.

But in the West Indies it permeated every part of our lives. We were these tiny islands, arcing up from South America, possession of which had changed hands over the years between the Spanish, French and Dutch before becoming British. I have an image of these men going off do the work of Empire. To enforce an economic system which, for three hundred years or so, was intimately tied to the furtherance of slavery. It needed men to do the terrible things that required. So public schools had to turn the boys that went into their maw into men capable of doing those things. Into good functionaries. That involved brutalising them, instilling in them a will to do what must be done. This was partly accomplished on the playing field. These men took cricket with them, a bubble of home. They arrived on unfamiliar shores with unfamiliar birds singing in unfamiliar trees. And they escaped into cricket. Here was this familiar space, of civilisation, of fairness, of spotless white uniforms when your other uniform surely was not. At first, it excluded those Black and brown men who toiled and died in the sun. But, gradually, they were allowed into the bubble too. They made it their own.

For some this will be far too pretty and blameless a conception of this story. Empires have always required inhumanity at their edges. Cricket was certainly a place where unconscionable hierarchies were enforced, but, as with all games, it was also a space for joy, for connection and communication. By the time I was a child, cricket was ours, to do as we wished with. Skill with the bat or the ball transcended all else. Men would become wistful when they talked about a particular drive that they had made as a younger man. There were men who our mothers would tell us not to go near. They were bad men, men who didn't have jobs. Who were in and out of trouble. There was the sense that it would somehow rub off on children. I would be told, 'Trevor, don't go near that man, he is a bad man.' But when he came to bat, as the brilliant chronicler of Trinidad and cricket C. L. R. James famously noted, they would draw back their curtains to watch him play. I have encountered West Indians in Moscow, or North Africa, who do fascinating jobs and lead fascinating lives – but it is cricket they really want to talk about: players, games, shots, moments, their eyes bright, their voices quick and loud.

In England, cricket is often invoked by a certain sort of propagandising nostalgist. The thwack of leather and willow and the ripple of applause on the village green often go alongside red telephone boxes, policemen wearing helmets and those other signifiers of a part-dimly remembered, part-imagined past. But growing up a child of Empire, cricket was a far more revolutionary pastime. When Dr Eric Williams championed the cause of West Indian self-determination, he referred to the fact that a few years earlier the West Indies had beaten the England cricket team for the first time. He went on to say, 'If we could beat the mother country at cricket, surely we can govern ourselves?' Cricket was a key way that the inhabitants of those disparate islands felt a sense of unified belonging outside of Empire. When you transition from a colonial mindset to an independent one, you need to work out what you are and what you stand for. What do you do? What don't you do? To have a sport so tied to the colonial endeavour, which you can then take owner-ship of and make your own, and then beat those colonisers? What a gift. Look at how we have mastery of the tools of our former masters. In Trinidad, two of the key tools were language and cricket.

So it is that cricket and the ideas and feelings swirling around it knit together the first thirty years of my life in Trinidad, and my life in England since. It was in listening to the glorious oratory of the cricket commentary and news broadcasts, and mouthing them to myself, that I found my voice. Like all Caribbean mothers, mine was insistent that I spoke the King's and (later) Queen's English. If my brother or I ever slipped into the speech we used when we played cricket we would be fixed with a look and a simple, 'What's that there?' She allied this requirement for us to speak 'properly' with a fierce education of the discrimination that confronted Jesse Owens or Joe Louis when they returned to the US and faced segregation. She would talk about the abomination of this system, until the two things became almost intertwined. It was those rhythms and cadences that echoed as I told Britain the stories that made up the news all those years later. There have been moments over the years when mothers have come up to me and told me, their eyes bright, how they would direct their children to look when I was on television. Because of what it meant if someone that looked like us was there, visible in that position. What might that mean? Though I assure you I was just a hack trying to get by, and I can't pretend I was ever guided by any higher purpose, what a lucky life to be someone who has been told that.

In a life defined by different sorts of talking, I have almost certainly spent more of my time talking about cricket than any other subject, perhaps fulfilling the oft-observed cliché that when women meet up they talk about their lives but when men meet they talk about sport. And what better sport is there than cricket to talk about?

Hooks, slashes, sweeps, cuts, drives, reverse sweeps, pulls, scoops, glances, square, short, driven, looping and slogged, nicked and hammered. Gully, silly point, silly mid-off, long-off and a thousand other words and phrases. Here was a game to satisfy the most shibboleth-hungry young boy.

Cricket is at the same time a hugely simple and endlessly complicated thing. For those used to the rhythms of other sports – the joyous bombast of football or the unrelenting symmetrical energy of basketball – cricket can seem strange. A game played with the metronome set to the wrong tempo.

It is a game of details. The shape of the finger as the ball is released; the precise bounce of that part of the ball on that exact part of the wicket. The moisture in the air; the moisture in the field. The precise angle of the blade of the bat. The single step taken the wrong way by the fielder; the weight on the wrong foot. The hand closing a fraction of a second too slowly. A flurry of electricity. The claim; the decision.

We go again. A procession of competence. Well-pitched ball and efficient bat. Cricket is a game of patiently waiting for the moment. The batsman waiting for the right ball. The fielders waiting for the improperly placed shot. To those who are not used to it, there is too much chaff, not enough wheat. But to the initiate, it is a rich landscape indeed.

It is an exercise in concentration, in sifting the moments that matter out of the quotidian and making sure you are ready to act when they arrive. It is all of life distilled.

Because of the rhythm of cricket, being in a crowd for a Test match just *feels* different. To be in a partisan crowd when a goal goes in is to be rocked and buffeted, flung about a tiny boat upon an ocean of angry joy or relief. It is a roar: the same sound I imagine that terrified Roman legionaries all those years ago.

In cricket, a good shot is more often admired. Each individual shot is a single thread in the tapestry of the match. This is often interpreted from the outside as evidence of the class of the crowd, perhaps more interested in their Fortnum & Mason hampers than the game. But it is relatively rare that a single shot carries within it the import a goal does in football. Across a five-day Test match there can be something like 2,700 balls bowled. To respond to a majority of them as definitive would be as futile as it was exhausting.

In most games, you stop playing if the ball changes. But cricket has made its peace with entropy. The ball's degradation is encouraged, cajoled into advantage. Cricket is a game of wholesale attrition. The pitch changes, wears away. But the players do too.

For those of us who worship at the altar of the wicket, it also somehow reveals something about those who play it. This is partly physical. To stand for hours on end on a hot summer's day in Sydney or Mumbai or Cape Town is no simple thing. But it is more than that. Cricket is a team game, but that compelling one-on-one battle lies at the heart of it. There is something essentially gladiatorial about the batter facing the bowler. I'm certain, at least, that the audience at the Colosseum would have understood a Curtly Ambrose bouncer. Until you have faced a decent-paced bowler 22 yards away, it is difficult to communicate the bravery it takes to be a batsman. It is not for nothing that both batsmen and outnumbered soldiers make stands. As the incomparable John Arlott put it, 'No one is so lonely as the batsman facing the bowler.'[1]

Can you keep facing those balls? Over and over? It finds the cracks in you. To be at wicket is to offer yourself up to a process of examination. As Neville Cardus famously said, 'A true batsman should in most of his strokes tell the truth about himself.'[2] To win a cricket match is both a physical and psychological battle. It is not for nothing that Rodney Hogg once described England captain Mike Brearley as having 'a degree in people'.[3] As we have seen the game change, the introduction of one-day internationals in 1971, then the 20 overs of T20 in 2003, T10, 100-ball, or whichever concentrated future version is concocted next, there have always been those lamenting the loss of the soul of cricket. But at every stage there has been an expansion of its audience. There is something in that central drama of bowler against batter that we can't look away from.

You encounter people, from time to time, who upon learning you are interested in sport are proud of their indifference. The 'it's-just-twenty-two-men-chasing-a-ball' crowd. To which I have often replied, in my head, 'Yes, and Verdi is just people striding about singing, and Shakespeare is just people saying words and pretending to be people they are not.' It is my opinion that to dismiss cricket is to dismiss life itself. The purity of purpose. That moment where all of the muddy variegated business of life comes down to an instant. Can you do it, or can you not? Perhaps, when you spend your professional life in things that are ambiguous and muddy and complicated, trying to find the story in them, sport produces certainty. Those of us who tell stories are drawn to the certainty of sport. There is nothing more relaxing than the sound of cricket through the radio, as bumblebees drift from flower to flower. There is a kind of magic there.

It is this magic that encourages love. Cricket produces an almost endless panoply of dramatic human narratives. Those narratives ran alongside the larger ones I reported in my day job. Watching, talking, reading and writing, cricket has been an anchor and a tether. Perhaps another reason for my connection to the news media comes from its function as a kind of umpire. At its best it holds the powerful to account as few things do. I think that one thing a proper news ecosystem does is connects us. It finds the ways that we are enmeshed and reminds us that no man, no woman, no person is an island. It is a great engine of commonality. It is no coincidence that the capture of the free press is the first thing on the agenda of repressive regimes. I am certainly not against citizen journalism. I think the fact that so many people are walking around with a functional camera in their pocket can be a marvellous thing. We should never stop having the conversation about how the news is created and shaped. The print media, especially, is incredibly concentrated in a small number of hands, who certainly want to advance their own interests much of the time. But the idea that the entirety of the media system is somehow corrupt and fundamentally untrustworthy is corrosive of democracy.

Perhaps that's what those voices through that little radio did all those years before for me. They brought these distant places a little closer. They showed how events around the world mattered and by extension how we matter to each other.

I was a boy born on one small island; I have spent the majority of my life on another. As I look around me, in times that feel so defined by division and separation – as we are bombarded with stories of invaders on boats, or foreign and threatening ideologies – it feels to me important to speak of the ties that bind. Of commonality and belonging and fellow feeling. Not because I ignore the very many problems we are faced with. But because I choose not to focus on them. When you live on an island, success is so often measured by the act of leaving. There is a central paradox at the heart of an island parent's love for their children. They both wish them great success, and know that this success makes it more likely they will one day wave them goodbye. Cricket is, for me, the thread strung between those two islands.

When I think about cricket, I think about belonging and joy. When I think about cricket, I think about love.

1

Cricket, Lovely Cricket

England versus West Indies, 29 June 1950

'Tre-vor. You are to come ho-ome!'

My earliest memories of cricket are being called home under duress on a Sunday evening, as I had not yet even started my homework. Huge, sprawling, fiercely competitive games with teams of indeterminate numbers that lasted from as soon after church as you were able to get away until the light finally gave out. In the Trinidadian climate, we could play almost all year round.

We played on tarmacadam roads baked soft in the sun, where cars would turn the other way, so as not to disturb us. Or we would find wasteland in between the gardens and smallholdings dotted in between the wooden houses of the village near Pointe-à-Pierre on the west coast of Trinidad where I grew up. We would improvise a pitch, our stumps a propped-up washboard. My younger brother was an expert crafter of cricket bats. These were not regulation, of course. Often, they would be the thicker sections of the branches of the fruit trees that grew around our house. There was some debate over whether the fruit of those trees belonged to us or our landlord, and my parents, always careful, urged us not to pick it. But at night we would reach out with a forked stick, draw the fruit-tree branches in and feast on the papayas, which were perhaps sweeter because of the tinge of transgression.

Not for us the careful, considered innings-building of an English player. We struck for the goat or pig shed, or into the sugar-cane field that marked our boundary. Our ball was a tennis ball, which we would soak in water to help it bounce more like a cricket ball.

The great footballer Johan Cruyff would attribute his remarkable control of the football to the odd angles the ball would bounce off the kerbs in the area of Amsterdam he grew up in playing football. My entire adult life, when I played cricket I would favour certain shots because these were the shots I favoured as a child. The bats that we played with, made from tree branches as they were, often had a serious bend in them. You were encouraged to hook, rather than rely on the unpredictable curved surface of the branch. Many of the strokes have never changed. I have always been a very bad leg player because if you hit it leg-side in our house, it would go into our particularly obstreperous neighbour's garden.

We would assign names from the West Indian national team. We would name ourselves after our players. And one summer, we had a crop of new heroes.

In the summer of 1950, the West Indies toured England, to play a four-match series. Old Trafford, Lord's, Trent Bridge, then the Oval. Magical faraway places. Although those childhood years are somewhat blurry, I remember the tour being a subject of discussion. I had been told that the final Test was set to finish at the Oval on my twelfth birthday. And I was desperate for the team to give me a present. But it was generally agreed that this was unlikely.

The West Indies had never won a match in England. They had only received Test status in 1928, but since then the score playing Test matches in England read: played six, drawn three, lost three. Though England had lost the series a couple of years earlier when they toured the West Indies, it was generally accepted that injuries to key English players rendered the result unrepresentative. At home and with more players to draw upon, not many gave us much of a chance.

It was agreed that we had three boys who could really bat: Clyde Walcott, Everton Weekes and Frank Worrell. They were all Barbadians, all born within a square mile of the Kensington Oval ground in Bridgetown, and, if you believed the legend, delivered by the same midwife.

Walcott, the youngest of the three, hit the ball so hard that it was said sensible fielders would get their hands out of the way. David Frith once referred to Walcott's batting as 'an unforgettable mix of silk and gently rolling thunder'.[4] Even off the back foot, he could generate this incredible force. And on the front foot, he could club an overpitched half-volley with something approaching savagery.

Weekes was said to be so graceful that the fielders would sometimes forget their duties and simply stand and admire his strokes. He once said that he only hit fours because, growing up, 'if you hit the ball in the air, you'd break someone's window'.[5]

Worrell seemed to wield his bat with a lightness and

delicacy; as he teased the ball over the boundary, the fielders following exhausted were always just a few paces behind. His cover-drives resembled the flick of an orchestra conductor's baton. He refused to hook because it offended his sense of the sanctity of the line. Neville Cardus said he didn't make a crude stroke in his entire career. He had signed as a professional for Radcliffe in the Central Lancashire League a couple of years before the 1950 series. He made such a good impression at Radcliffe that, in 1964, they renamed a street near the cricket ground Worrell Close. But he pared this delicacy with a stubborn set of principles. After refusing to travel on a tour of India in 1948 unless they improved the stipend for the players, he had been branded a 'Cricket Bolshevik'. Together, Walcott, Weekes and Worrell would become known as the three Ws.

That 1950 team was braided from the complicated strands of the region.

Cricket had originally been brought to the islands by white colonial officials and planters. Early on it was exclusively their pastime. But bowling was no easy thing in the heat, so enslaved people began to bowl. And little by little cricket put down roots. There were cricket clubs on each island, initially only for white people, a situation that lasted until after slavery was abolished. The first tournament between the varying colonies took place in 1891 between Trinidad, Barbados and Demerara, which became British Guiana (and later Guyana).

Black cricket clubs formed and played between themselves on Saturdays. But as C. L. R. James described, there remained complicated networks of class and race that went along with playing for each club. Some were still just for white people, some the 'brown-skinned middle class', as he put it.[6] Charles Ollivierre was the first Black West Indian player to play county cricket for Derbyshire, in 1901. But even as late as 1950 the captain of the West Indies was always white. The top order comprised almost always white batters. The West Indies Cricket Board of Control was entirely composed of upper-class whites. Everton Weekes said that the board saw players like him in the same way 'that estate owners saw field hands'.[7] It didn't matter that there were better players who were Black, the team had to have a white captain.

It is not hard to unpick this. You could trust a Black man to run, to throw, to hit. But to organise a field? Devise a strategy? To be a leader of himself and others? Of course not. The year that I had been born, the two obvious candidates for the captaincy had been Learie Constantine, commonly agreed to have been the finest cricketer the West Indies has ever produced, or the hugely talented George Headley. Instead, the job was given to Rolph Grant, a not particularly gifted player but white and a gentleman, so the right sort for it. Learie Constantine would write in his memoirs of the 'whites only' dances held after matches with England. Things weren't quite as bad by 1950 – and the captain John Goddard and opening batsmen like Jeffrey Stollmeyer were extremely good players in their own right. But the balance of which players, of which backgrounds and from which islands was always a topic of conversation, and it felt like it was about more than just sporting prowess.

We were to have two young spin bowlers on the tour who had only played two first-class matches before setting off for England: the Jamaican Alf Valentine, who was twenty, and the Trinidadian Sonny Ramadhin, who turned twenty-one a month before the first Test. Spin bowling hadn't been a huge part of West Indian cricketing heritage. The previous generation had been more associated with pace where bowling was concerned. Both Valentine and Ramadhin were so green that the story was later told that they had to have the concept of signing autographs explained to them on the journey to England. Sonny was the first man of Indian origin to play for the West Indies. Christopher Columbus had named the island of Trinidad after the Holy Trinity in 1498. But when he sailed past there were already a number of groups of indigenous people living there, predominantly Arawak and Carib. They called the island Ka-iri or Iere. At first it was the Spanish settlers who came, but this was gradually expanded to any Catholic European, which then attracted a great many French and some Irish Catholics. For hundreds of years the island produced sugar as first the indigenous population and then hundreds of thousands of enslaved Central and West Africans were worked to death in the sun. Everyone worked: men, women, children and the elderly. Sugar was hard, physical work at every stage, and a third of enslaved Africans died within three years of arriving in the Caribbean.

Trinidad was formally ceded to the British in 1802. The beneficiaries of the sugar money changed but the dynamic did not. Slavery had been abolished just over a hundred years before I was born, but we were still in touching distance of it. You would sometimes meet people who remembered their older relatives telling stories of when they were enslaved. When he was a child, the Trinidadian legend Learie Constantine would remember his grandfather leaning back in the sun and looking at him and thinking that when he had been that age, he had been enslaved. His grandmother too. My surname is McDonald. Somewhere in my father's family history we must have been enslaved on a plantation owned by a McDonald family. If you were one of that plantation's boys, you were a McDonald boy. (At various points, my sister has been interested in trying to get to the bottom of our exact ancestry. But I have never felt particularly interested. The only thing I know for certain is that it once got me bought a lot of drinks as a younger man in a bar in Glasgow.)

Slavery in all British territories was abolished in 1838. As the majority of newly freed Africans refused to work, the British had to act quickly to ensure labour. They tried Portugal, China and America, but in the end it was to be India that supplied the bulk of the labour. It is estimated that between 1845 and 1917 more than one hundred and fifty thousand indentured labourers were brought from colonial India to Trinidad by the British to work on the sugar estates.

Sonny Ramadhin's people were brought to work the sugar-cane of the Picton Estate, which was about four hour's walk from my village. Sonny would recall that when he was thirteen, he would practise bowling at the estate and the secretary would put a penny on the wicket, which he could win if he hit it. By the time I was growing up, sugar had been supplanted as the main economic product by the discovery of oil. But those with Indian heritage tended to be the shopkeeper class. I often thought my father's side of the family, who came from Grenada, where there had been a similar movement of population, must have had some of this heritage. A rope woven from indentured servitude and slavery. The difference between the two, of course, being the former is finite, the other designed to last for ever. Such are the subtle but important gradations of colonial history. Indentured servants sometimes got land when their contract was up. This gave a small economic leg up to those from that background – and promoted friction between the communities. At the very least, when India played the West Indies at cricket the island seemed in many ways to split in half. Our village suddenly had conflicting allegiances. When the great Indian batsman Nari Contractor was hit on the skull by a ball from Charlie Griffith in 1962 it was something akin to a diplomatic incident. But it was more than cricket; that diversion of paths between slavery and servitude indicated a deeper division. My mother was always of the opinion that those shopkeepers of Indian descent had to have more of an eye kept on them and couldn't be fully trusted. When I pointed out that Dad was almost certainly part Indian, she said, 'Your father is entirely different.'

This young player, Sonny, who was ten years older than me and who grew up half a day's walk from where I lived, was here, halfway around the world. Understandably, when that series began, round our way there was a natural extra focus on him. How would this young man and the team face up to the challenge of the English? Early signs were not entirely promising.

The weather was cold and rainy in Manchester, and the players seemed shocked by it. Though the pitch suited spin bowlers and the debutants did well – Alf took 11 wickets and Sonny took 4 across both innings – the West Indian batsmen were unable to deal with the English spinners, and England won the first Test by a bruising 202 runs. Things seemed to be proceeding according to the script. I reported the day's action to my father as we sat by the riverbank, watching our fishing rods.

When I wasn't playing cricket, or at school, I treasured the hours spent fishing with my father. We would walk past the fields of sugar-cane to the muddy river closest to our house, bend bobby pins and, using earthworms, fish from the banks. In that way that fishing provokes, we would talk about what we saw, the bob of the fishing rod and the river in front of us, but also of our days, of what we had done and were going to do. My father was not a voluble man, but he communicated his interest and his care.

My father and I would catch flathead and catfish, sometimes lobster. My father was a gentle, generous man, who believed utterly in the power of education as a passport to a better life and wanted it for his children. We would take the fish up and my mother would cook them with rice and peas. My mother's cooking was a miracle in that it didn't matter how many people turned up unannounced, the food would always expand to feed them. If I turned up at lunchtime with a friend, she would welcome them to the table. She used to say that we must always be generous to strangers in case we missed out on 'the glorious chance of entertaining angels'. I still think that one of the finer phrases I have ever heard. There was still rationing when I was growing up and there was never enough food to go around. In response to their worries about our imperfect diet, my parents were firm believers in the health-cure sellers who would visit our village. One that I cannot recall without wincing to this day was the whale-oil man. He would announce his arrival in a loud nasal voice: 'Whale oil, come get whale oil.' And then my brother and sisters and I would be forced to gag down the viscous fishy liquid. Whatever you are currently imagining, it was worse, and made cod liver oil seem like ambrosia in comparison. So we developed strategies to get rid of him. I would lower my voice and call out, 'Get away from here or I'll let the dogs go,' in order to scare him away before he had the chance to replenish our supply.

Our village, and Trinidad more broadly, was full of people from all sorts of backgrounds. African, Indian, Syrian, Chinese. Because Trinidad had oil we attracted people from the other islands. We always thought that the Jamaicans acted like we were yokels, because their island was by far the biggest. My father was born in Grenada and always believed that they spoke the finest English in the region. But we were a hub of a tiny wheel. Even Jamaica, while the largest island, had a population a little smaller than that of Manchester and Liverpool as they were at that time combined. The population of Barbados, which has produced so many of the most talented West Indian cricketers of all time, was more like two hundred and twenty thousand people, about the size of Portsmouth in Britain at the time. We were, by any metric, tiny islands.

Though there was little money and life was by no means easy, we were also dimly aware that there were people for whom our island was something they escaped their real life to experience at great expense. I would get home from school and see the tide rising and I would go home and change, then go swimming. I spent so much time outside. I would go out into the bush and read books with the kingbirds trilling in the trees above me. This was life. I'm not sure we ever really longed for holidays, not that we would have been able to afford them, because we lived in what was in many ways an idyll. To pick a sweet Julie mango from a tree, warmed from the sun, and eat it. To cook fish you caught yourself half an hour before (or bring it to your mother to cook, at least). School, fishing and cricket. That was almost my entire life. And for those almost eight weeks in the summer of 1950, it felt as if every day there was a new revelation from the team in England.

Twelve days after the first Test and down at Lord's in London the weather was better. The West Indies batted first and got to 326. Then England. And Sonny and Alf destroyed them. Alf took 4 wickets, Sonny 5 as England struggled to 151 runs. Used to bowling on the hard pitches of the West Indies, or on what is known as matting – a playing surface of jute or cocoa fibre used where turf does not willingly grow – Sonny would later remember how in the damper English air the ball was almost 'turning square'. In the second innings, the West Indies batsman seemed energised, especially Clyde Walcott who hit 168, as the West Indies added another 425. This left England needing 601 to win and two days to survive for the draw. And, by God, they tried to grind it out, and over the next 140-odd overs they kept the scoreboard turning, though Sonny took 6 and Alf 3. They made it to 274. And when their final batsman was out LBW, some of the West Indians came on to the pitch with musical instruments creating what John Arlott described as 'an atmosphere of joy such as Lord's had never known before'. The West Indies had won by 326 runs.

Sonny would later remember running to the dressing room, where the captain John Goddard got out a crate of his own rum, Goddard's Gold Braid.

The West Indian fans were smartly dressed, as they had been when they'd arrived in the country. It was both a sign of respect but also of self-defence – perhaps if you were dressed as gentle people, you would be treated gently. None of us heard that final moment live at the time, because the BBC did not have a team there due to their need to cover the tennis at Wimbledon. But I heard fragments, as men read out match reports. We pieced it together like detectives in the days afterwards.

The great Trinidadian calypsonians Lord Kitchener and Lord Beginner wrote a calypso to celebrate. Over the fol- lowing days and weeks, every time I could, I snuck to my friend's house to listen to the matches. We would win at Trent Bridge by 10 wickets and at the Oval by an innings and 56 runs. Across the whole tour, Valentine took 33 wickets and Ramadhin 26.

And suddenly every boy who thought he had a decent spin bowl in him wanted to be Sonny Ramadhin or Alf Valentine. And the adults talked with excitement about what it meant. The following year, *Wisden* named Sonny Ramadhin, Alf Valentine, Everton Weekes and Frank Worrell as players of the year. I remember it as a time suffused with sunlight and pride.

However, at home my prolonged absences at various points had not gone unnoticed. My mother and father decided that it was too distracting for me to go to someone else's house to listen to cricket. They didn't want my schoolwork to suffer.

My father, as noted, was a total believer in education as the key to unlocking the life he wanted for us. He had worked for many years at the oil refinery. Dirty, hard, sometimes dangerous work. He watched as a new graduate from Cambridge would be parachuted into the office as his boss, without ever getting their hands dirty. He would never have the opportunity to be at that desk, and he knew it was because he didn't have the right education. My parents had such good hearts that the discipline came not from fear or enforcement but from us not wanting to do anything that would disappoint them. My mother loved to quote Longfellow:

> Lives of great men all remind us,
> We can make our lives sublime,
> And, departing, leave behind us
> Footprints on the sands of time;

I remember not really understanding what the sands of time were. But from the context she used it in, I knew it meant something about trying as hard as you possibly could. It is a classic joke of a West Indian upbringing that a child comes back with 96 per cent as his test result and shows his parent proudly. And they say, 'What about the other four?!' But it was certainly true of my family.

There were about eight of us in what was known as the 'exhibition class', which was where the students they thought had potential were placed. I was very much there through work, rather than talent. There were tests every week. And if in one month I did well on all four of the tests, my father said he would buy me a bicycle. I got three good results and missed the final one by a couple of marks. I did not get the bicycle. From time to time, we would be invited to explain how to work through a complicated mathematical theorem on the board. Most of the time I successfully avoided it, but on one occasion I stood in front of the class hesitantly explaining what I thought I needed to do, only for the teacher to say, 'Sit down, McDonald. I've never heard such rubbish in my whole life.' I was good at English and history and geography. I liked words and stories. Our parents' and the school's ambitions for us were for education to open the doors to the professional classes: lawyers, doctors, engineers. I hated exams. It felt as if the majority of it was just a memory and rote-learning exercise. Two of the boys got a scholarship to secondary school but I did not, and my poor father had to pay.

We were a family of four children – me, the oldest, then my younger brother, JC, then my sisters, Lynette and Eunice. On one salary the numbers didn't make sense. On Friday afternoons, if my father was doing one of the shifts, which took him late into the day, I would be sent down to the oil refinery to pick up money so that my mother could buy food for the evening. Then we would go around to all of the shops we had bought food from on credit over the course of the week and pay our bills. By the time we'd done that there would be no money left. That feeling of an envelope of money emptying as soon as it was full is not one you ever forget. My other job was to queue on a Saturday to buy the cheap offcuts left over from the more expensive joints of meat.

I remember once that there was a strike at the oil refinery. But, though he cared deeply about their cause, my father could not afford to strike. So, he would wear his clothes for dinner and then sneak into work. I must have been nine or ten. We would call out, 'Goodbye, Father. Enjoy your dinner,' to add to the subterfuge. We would lay awake, worried that he would be discovered and beaten up. I could tell that he wished he could strike but he had four children to feed.

Presumably, businesses having to pay a wage at all meant an increased cost that hadn't been necessary for previous generations of factory owners in Trinidad. So, they were slow to advance pay and conditions compared to other places.

We absorbed the necessity for hard work through watching the actions of our parents. I'm not sure anything needed to be said. There were no great clashes about it that I remember. My brother and sister and I knew where the boundaries were and didn't want to disappoint our parents. We watched and saw a life of hard work, which never seemed to be quite enough. We had a market garden. We kept pigs. At one point my father was a cobbler. My mother's ability to make ends meet was remarkable. But, even so, my father was constantly working. I am not entirely sure exactly how my parents met. I suspect my father met his future wife at the oil refinery when she was a servant for one of the expats who was a senior figure there. It is one of the great tragedies of human life that when they are there to ask, we are often too young to be interested in such things. By the time you are ready to enquire about the lives of your parents, they are no longer with you. My father believed in working hard, in doing what you said you'd do. In taking responsibility. And we all grew up believing that was the default. If I have ever been a good colleague, it was because I replicated the behaviour of my father. On some mornings when it rained, one of my father's colleagues would pick me up. 'Hop in, Mr McDonald's son.' There was the sense that my father was liked and respected, and to feel that made me feel good, made me want to repeat what he did and perhaps I would be liked and respected too. He would be constantly telling us stories of our neighbour's children, or nieces or nephews who had gone on to be doctors or engineers. At the time, I couldn't understand why he thought I would care about these people who I did not know. But looking back now, I think he was providing us with a constant sense that achievement was possible, even probable. He was expanding our horizon, even though we didn't know it at the time. He was giving us a view of ourselves and our place in the world that he had not been given. He would find them and point at them and say, 'That could be you.' He genuinely believed that striving hard enough made anything possible. And somehow I internalised that and translated it into, 'Why not me?'

I was always told as a schoolboy to respect everyone around us. I remember, quite often, I would be wandering down the street, probably lost in some mild worry about schoolwork I hadn't completed, and I would forget to greet someone we knew in the street. Without fail, my father would note, 'Mr Roberts said you passed him in the street and didn't say hello.' We were taught to be respectful, to say good morning or good afternoon to everyone we passed. If my father saw a teacher, he would ask for an impromptu school report, and if it was anything other than fulsome praise I would be kept in for further study, which would eat into my time to play cricket. He was always clear that if you ever got into trouble, these were the people who would come to your rescue. When anyone in our village died, the whole family would dress in their best and go to the funeral. That was a way of showing respect. Our father took such great interest in our lives. He didn't talk much. But he viewed most situations with a quiet equanimity. It strikes me now that he had that quiet authority that the cricket captains I most admired had – a sense that they don't need to say it because they lived it.

It is often said of someone that they would give you the shirt from their back, but in my father's case that was true. And he'd probably express regret that it did not fit you better too. He took me to my first day at school. He was a man who I never saw face the world with bitterness or anger. He was firm and he was demanding. My mother was exacting in the standards she demanded of me and my siblings. She was a woman who thought and talked with the clarity of scripture. She took a dim view of calypsos and dancing and things of that nature. We had a wind-up gramophone, but my brother and I would take it a little way away from the house to a kind of tunnel and we'd listen to the calypsos that we knew our mother wouldn't approve of. There was, it seemed, a constant process of ensuring that you were not drawn into the wrong crowd, who would infect you with indolence and drag you back into the morass of humanity.

Nobody in our village had much money. And there could be grudges held for generations. There were fights sometimes after the rum shop closed on a Friday night. These could get violent and even involve cutlasses or knives, but guns were a real rarity. There was marijuana, but perhaps due to my caution, no one I knew smoked it (or at least not around me).

But it was the natural corollary of a community that size,

one relatively fixed in terms of incomings and outgoings, that people knew each other. There was a general sense of consequences to actions that were deemed to be antisocial. The old adage 'I know your dad' was no empty threat. It was drummed into me that whatever we had, we would share it if it was needed. Part of life was to host your neighbours. If someone arrived in our village and knocked on someone's door, asking for a neighbour, the thing to do was to go and walk them to the house, not give them directions. It was a small thing, but it was one of the loops of community that bound us to each other.

There was no space for rudeness. When I was young that resulted in what felt like an almost painful smallness; a kind of suffocating feeling of being watched. But now when I look back, I can see some of the more positive aspects of it. We were pretty poor. But my mother would often give me packages of food to take over to our neighbours who had less. I once said to her, 'We don't have much. Why are we giving it to them?' She replied, 'They've got another little one just arrived.' I said, 'Well, maybe they should stop having babies.' My mother fixed me with a look I shall never forget. I don't now recall if she went through with washing my mouth out but she certainly threatened it and I believed her. She was a remarkable lady. I never knew my mother's father. But I know that he gave speeches at village fêtes. He gave her a great fondness for language and fine turns of phrase. It was partly, of course, the Bible, which she read and quoted from.

My parents had a very strong sense of what we needed to survive and perhaps thrive in the world. They knew that education and working hard was the bedrock. If you reached for the stars, you might just touch the tops of the trees. To be given whatever ingredients it requires to keep going when you encounter adversity – as a young person, you may not always be grateful for it. But when you get on in life and meet people without it, you realise that it is the greatest gift you can be given.

The family my father did odd jobs for had two boys not far in age from my brother and me. One day, when we had cast our line into whichever muddy river we were fishing in, my father said, 'We should get the Finlayson boys to come fish here.' I looked at him and said, 'Dad, they're white, they're not going to want to come here. We don't have a car. How will they get here?'

'I'll go and fetch them on the bus.'

My brother and I looked at each other. I am almost certain one of us asked if white people got the bus. I had certainly never seen any on the buses I took. We rolled our eyes at our father and his infinite but surely misplaced faith in humanity. I remember being a little worried on his behalf that he would be embarrassed by their response. But a few days later, at the end of the dusty track, there he was with the two Finlayson boys, who had got the bus and came down to fish with us in the brown water. We sat for hours, muttering about potential strikes and where to cast. Then they thanked us. My father just smiled and said we'd best get the fish back to mother, then went with them to catch the bus home. He didn't see any distinction between people. It has become a watchword for those who deny the impact of race to say that they don't see race. My father certainly saw it but was just not inter-ested by it. He would back himself to talk to and get on with anyone. It wasn't long before those boys were bundled off to public school in Scotland. Both of them became doctors and we didn't see them any more. But, fifty years later, I met them again and we talked about our childhoods. We talked about my father.

In a life full of lucky events, the first and greatest was to be brought into the world by my parents, the two most wonderful people in the world. To be loved, to know you are loved, but that they have great expectations of you. They lived long enough that they knew I hadn't mucked things up entirely. There is still not a day that goes by that I do not give thanks for my parents. I have missed them every day since they have been gone.

We moved home a few times when I was a child, from one rented house to another, always in the same area. The house I remember best was on a steep hill. I remember that the fruit delivery truck would slow right down as it took the sharp turn at the bottom of the hill, then struggle to come back up to speed as it went up the hill. If you were quick, and brave, you could catch up to it and lift boxes of fruit out the back, to take home, or sell to the neighbours. I wish I could say it was my morality, but the truth is I was never brave enough to do it. Even my mother turned a blind eye to the provenance of the 'good mangoes' that would, from time to time, turn up at suspiciously low prices after the fruit truck had been heard groaning past our house.

Their solution to my listening to the cricket at my friend's house was to buy a radio. It was a huge, cumbersome thing with a large, heavy battery, but it did the trick.

And it was to change my life. It meant, for the first time,

that I was exposed to cricket commentary properly. This was, after all, the era of John Arlott, a published poet. And perhaps it was cricket's roots in the polite barbarity of the English public school system that paradoxically connects it to beauty. Cricket commentary and cricket journalism never feels far from poetry. But it was Arlott who people would declaim as if it were poetry. Partly we loved him because he didn't seem partisan in his admiration. Some commentators seemed to only view their own as possessing the requisite quality to be truly great. But he seemed to put that aside and see greatness in moments, in players and shots, wherever he found it. But he also just had the most wonderful turn of phrase. Once, he described a stroke as 'played so late as to be a sparrow's blink of being posthumous'; another time a bowler's distinctive run-up reminded him of 'Groucho Marx chasing a pretty waitress'. He described fielders as 'scattering like missionaries to far places'. How can you not love the mind of someone who greeted the English batsman George Mann being bowled out by the South African Tufty Mann with, 'What we have here is a clear case of Mann's inhumanity to Mann'? Or someone who described Peter Loader's capering delight at getting a hat-trick against the West Indies by describing him 'jumping all over the place, like a monkey on a stick'? The great cricketing journalist Frank Keating described Arlott as 'the most celebrated British voice after Churchill'.

All this was about the same time I discovered that I enjoyed reading poetry out loud. The rhythm of the words. The cadences. The music of it. At school we would sit out under the trees and recite Keats, Byron, Yeats and Tennyson; thirty children raucously chanting 'The Charge of the Light Brigade'.

I have no idea what passers-by thought. I would come home and lie for hours, listening to events halfway around the world. I began to listen to the news too. More, different words, but they also conjured pictures in my mind. Growing up in a British colony, the mother country was where it all happened. It was their poets we read. I wonder now about my classroom colleagues who did not revel in poetry: perhaps they would have done so if the words they read in their books sounded more like the words they heard in the street. If we had been taught Trinidadian history alongside British history, what might it have done for our sense of ourselves?

Perhaps that is an impossible question to answer. Because it was their history we were taught as our history; their news that filled the papers and then the radio. Consequently, there was a general feeling that nothing of consequence occurred on the islands. In those places where they were required to have clocks with the time in various cities around the world, Port of Spain was not one of them. A natural consequence of any sort of excellence was that you would be brought to the mother country. There was thought to be a smallness about wanting to stay on the island. To be a child of the British Empire in that part of the world was to feel you were very much at the edge of a wheel, with London at its centre. The gravitational pull to the mother country was strong. As I listened to these places – Geneva, Paris, Berlin, London: exotic cold places, full of greys and browns and beiges – I began to conceive of how big the world was. And that there was a life that involved journalists meeting politicians and diplomats, and interviewing them. I also was rather drawn to the idea that such journalists were probably put up in nice hotels. I had recently learned of these, and rather liked the sound of them. Those things were distant dreams for boys round our way. I began the habit of talking to teachers about global events. I would have these long, I'm sure astonishingly rambling, questions for them, which through their kindness and patience they answered. Though I'm not sure I would have used the word, I discovered I was interested in politics. In how things happened, in who got to make decisions. In how people around the world found out about those decisions. I was still a timid, bookish child, but I felt, right at the edges of my apprehension, that there was a world to learn about. Looking back, perhaps the bravest thing I ever did was begin to imagine that I could do what I heard those men on the radio doing.

And it all began with that summer, with those young men, whose names we would call out as our own, who became our childhood heroes.

2

'Oh, it's a Tie!'

Brisbane Test, 9 December 1961

'Trevor, you have everything you need?' The radio station manager looked at me. I couldn't help feeling as if this was potentially a rather large question, and must have thought about it for just a little too long. 'For later?' He gestured around us at the tiny room, the surfaces cramped with papers, files and coffee cups. I nodded. I had a flask full of coffee to keep me going. I had a notepad. I had the youthful enthusiasm of a twenty-one-year-old in his first job. I had made it my policy to say yes to everything on the advice of my boss, Ken Gordon. Perhaps I was predisposed to the advantages of being a good all-rounder.

Secondary school had passed by in somewhat of a blur, most of which had been spent with me worrying about exams and then what I would do with my exams. When I had been sixteen, I had tried to drop Latin, only to be told that I had to have Latin if I wanted to be a doctor or a lawyer. I told them I didn't want to be either, and they looked at me like I'd started taking all of my clothes off and dancing around the room. By that time, I had an inkling of what I *did* want to do. Partly as a strategy to get out of the fifth or so maths class of the week, I had started up a little radio station at my secondary school. The last class before school broke up on a Friday, I was allowed to broadcast to the school over the public address system. Each week, I would diligently copy down stories from the BBC World Service in my notebook and then repeat them to my classmates. I sometimes got people to be interviewed on it. I did it because I enjoyed it, rather than out of any generous desire to educate my contemporaries.

A few years later, I would learn that the existence of my 'show' had spread beyond my school to other schools. I particularly remember a former student at the girls' school twinned with ours who told me that they had all been terribly impressed to hear about what I was doing. I couldn't help but wish that someone had told me at the time.

But, in the meantime, I still had to do the exams, which would potentially unlock college. I knew I was not academically gifted enough to get one of the small handful of scholarships to Oxford or Cambridge that were so prized by island parents. I had started to study law and international relations but, if I was honest, I was keen to work as soon as I could. I was keen to get out into the world, away from my small community where it felt as if everyone's eyes were upon me.

Towards the end of secondary school I had started to go to the Queen's Park Oval in Port of Spain. My parents were always terribly protective and would only let me travel the 35 miles there with adult supervision: I was only allowed to go with one of my father's friends from the oil refinery. I still remember the first time I went. The excitement about going into the city. The drive there, as the gaps between the houses got smaller. The cars everywhere. But also bicycles and horse-drawn carts with barrels, their drivers stood up with the reins. The traffic policemen in their high-waisted shorts and hats, waving the traffic this way and that. Everywhere people striding about. The men in shirtsleeves and hats. The women in dresses. Women with baskets of fruit on their heads. One basket piled with dead chickens. Different buildings. Taller, broader, more imposing. I had no language to conceive of architecture, just that the buildings were different. And then the ground itself. So big and grand. The pavilion. The hills rising in the background. I knew that my ticket to the world started in Port of Spain. And I was desperate to get there.

Unbeknownst to me, news of my school 'radio station' had already made it to Port of Spain and Radio Trinidad, where an English woman called Val Douglas had heard about it. Radio Trinidad broadcast shows on the weekend for younger people, and as part of that they interviewed young people on the island. So, I was asked to appear as a guest on one of those shows. I am certain that I bored everyone I met telling them that I wanted to be a journalist. But it meant that when they had a scheme to bring someone new to the station, I heard about it, and they already knew a little of me. I applied and, to my astonishment, I was swiftly accepted. I moved to a small apartment in Port of Spain. My father, as he had on my first day of school, took me to my first day of work. He got up incredibly early in the morning to get me there.

Radio Trinidad was owned by Rediffusion, a British company. In Britain they essentially took the BBC signal and re-diffused it, so people could pick it up more easily. But in Trinidad that hadn't been possible because of the technology, and so they broadcast original programming to the island. There was a constant stream of British undergraduates who would come to Trinidad for work and a wonderful couple of years in the sun. It wasn't particularly easy to get a job at Rediffusion as a Trinidadian. The fact I had was the subject of no little curiosity among those Englishmen. It was in many ways a white establishment, and when I applied there wasn't a huge queue of native Black Trinidadian broadcasters. My boss, Ken Gordon, would go on to write a book about his life detailing the discouragement he faced for working in radio as a Black Trinidadian. Fundamentally the radio was seen as a white career. People from England who fancied working on the radio in Trinidad for a couple of years were just ahead in the queue. I don't necessarily think there was any conscious malice; it was just the way that it had always been. There was a kind of a feedback loop. It was the way it had always been and this made it all the more likely that it was how it always would be.

Over those first weeks and months, I read the news. I played records. I would go to the airport to meet celebrities coming in. They would quite often stop over in Trinidad if they were on their way somewhere else. I loved interviewing people: I once accidentally stepped on Sammy Davis Jr's foot and further annoyed him by asking questions about the Rat Pack instead of what he wanted to talk about, which was his life away from the Rat Pack. I would take myself out with a tape recorder and get the interview. I remember the Guyanese premier, Cheddi Jagan, once making the plane wait for him because he had promised me an interview. I learned that you can leave behind all of your nervousness and confidently ask the questions. I also learned that lots of people found this sort of thing onerous, but to me it felt like the bare minimum of work to do. One of my roles early on was to go into the technical chamber and start up all the equipment in the morning. I am astonished that I was given that responsibility. I was always petrified that I would somehow set it on fire.

I volunteered to commentate on tennis, and even water polo. I commentated on boxing, until one particularly vicious punch landed the red corner's gumshield into my lap, along with a decent volume of bloody spittle. That was the end of my professional association with blood sports. I commentated on football. I learned how to commentate on horse racing. I had never been to a track – my parents associated it with immorality. You have to memorise the colours and speak very quickly. Races in Trinidad could be very short – five furlongs. And twelve horses. I met a racehorse owner a couple of years later who recognised my voice as I ordered at a bar, asked my name and proceeded to berate me for never reading his horse's name out before the race ended. I apologised profusely. What my critic failed to tell me was that his horse never left the gate.

Rediffusion wanted Radio Trinidad to be a profit-generating endeavour. To that purpose we had a sales manager whose job it was to sell advertising space to the island businesses. He was a charismatic and utterly forceful man who could sell honey to a bee. When I started doing cricket commentaries, the plum gig was, of course, the Test matches. But there was a strict hierarchy, and there were those far above me in the pecking order who put dibs in on that. So I resolved to cut my teeth on the local matches, even though I was far less interested in them. This sales manager was so good at his job that he would sell sponsorship even to the least of these clashes. Our programming was supported by advertisements for everything from potions that encouraged regular bowel movements, to milk powder and funeral parlours. I remember there was one match I had been put down to commentate on and I really didn't have much interest in doing so. But the sales manager had sold sponsorship, so I had to. It got to about 11 a.m. and the sky opened in a deluge. It was biblical. A dull white-grey sky, the sort that signals the rain has dug in and will not be dissuaded. I bumped into our sales manager on the staircase. He looked at his watch and said, 'You almost ready to head to the game?' I was unable to hide the glee in my eyes as I gestured outside to the slate sky, the trees bending under the force of the rain, and signalled how much I wished I could, but God had intervened. Without smiling he looked at me and said, 'I have sold that game. I'm going home now. But when I am inside, I'm going to switch my radio on. And when I do so, rain or no rain, I want to hear commentary.' And with that he left. I was unsure if he was joking or not. And that was something that followed me the whole of my time at Radio Trinidad.

I had aspirations, of course, to be an international cricket commentator. We would listen to English county cricket on a Saturday afternoon. We had a knowledge of their cricket that rivalled British fans': there were rivalries of Yorkshire versus Lancashire; in our teens, we had an expansive knowledge of who had made a hundred for Glamorgan the previous week: Len Hutton and Trevor Bailey, and so on. I heard many times of pilgrimages from the West Indies to these legendary places. It pleases me to think of these West Indian men walking about the streets of Birmingham, Leeds or Manchester, starry-eyed, as if it was their Graceland. There was a perhaps apocryphal story that West Indian men would drive their heavily pregnant wives to Yorkshire so that their children could be born there and thereby keep alive the possibility of their playing for Yorkshire, thus fulfilling the club law that was to stand from 1863 until the mid 1990s.

I couldn't get onto the commentary roster officially. My two bosses were also cricket nuts, so they didn't want me muscling them out of the way. Instead, they tasked me with trying to get the great John Arlott as a commentator for one of the Tests. I wrote him an impassioned letter with our offer of a fee and the promise of a case of what I was told was good wine to convince him. He never replied, so I can only assume that neither was up to snuff.

To accelerate my career as a cricket commentator, I hit upon a scheme. The great cricket journalist Jim Swanton used to take tours out to the islands and would play in a fixture in Grenada. I called the Grenadian radio station who would be covering it and told them that I was a distinguished cricket commentator in Trinidad: could I come and commentate there? One of them was somehow under the misapprehension that I was the lead commentator for Radio Trinidad. I didn't correct him. When I came back to Trinidad my bosses said they'd heard me and that I wasn't bad. In fact, the Englishman who managed Radio Trinidad had heard me and had reportedly said that they were going to try to have 'more Trevor' in their cricket coverage.

It was also one of my responsibilities to read the death announcements. People would pay money to hear, 'John Smith died last Tuesday at the age of eighty-one. He is survived by his wife Jane and his two adoring children Tommy and Suzie of Suffolk, England.' Woe betide you got the names wrong. Relatives would come into the studio to complain. It was prime advertising real estate, as everyone listened to it. No births or marriages. Just deaths. I would return to my small apartment exhausted but astonished by how much I was learning. I no longer really had the time to play cricket, but I followed it at every opportunity that I could. Though I was starting to get a little known on the radio, my parents would never let me get too big for my boots. I would go home for dinner now and again and they would say, 'Oh, Mrs Smith heard you on the radio the other day. She said you sounded English.' But that would be it.

In Port of Spain I saw another example of Trinidadian love of language when people who were unemployed lined up to hear court cases. They did this to listen to the language. Then they would repeat this language back that evening. I would be reporting in court and jostling with them to get a seat. They were fascinated by what the right words in the right order could unlock. It is a commonly observed pattern of former colonies that language is one of the master's key tools that the people want to use.

I bought a blue car to drive myself about, and people knew me as Trevor from the radio with the blue car. I was not paid a huge amount, but I sent money back to my parents. My father left the oil refinery when he reached a certain stage, but then he started making shoes, employing a couple of people locally. He didn't stop working hard.

When it transpired in December 1960 that we needed someone to listen to the West Indies and Australia on the commentary feed coming from Brisbane, Australia – in order to be able to update the island as soon as was humanly possible – it came to be that I was tasked with listening to the final day's play of the third Test at Brisbane so I could put together a report for the early morning news bulletin. Because of the time difference this would mean starting at around midnight and working through potentially till six or seven in the morning. The Brisbane Test was to be the first of a five-match tour of Australia, taking in Melbourne, Sydney and Adelaide then finishing up with a game back in Melbourne.

There was a general feeling around the world that the last ten years had seen a kind of tightening into safety first where Test cricket was concerned. But in Australia and the West Indies there were two teams that had a commitment to entertaining the fans. It was reported that Richie Benaud, who was working as a columnist for one of the Australian newspapers, bumped into Frank Worrell at the airport. As they said their goodbyes, Benaud said, 'I hope it's a great summer,' to which Worrell replied with a smile, 'We'll have a lot of fun anyway.' There was, at this time, thought to be a kind of brittle quality to the West Indies: mercurial but liable to crack under pressure. Our fielding was suspect. Our mentality second rate. Whereas Australia were a hard-nosed winning machine. They were a nation determined to prove their cricketing validity with every match they played. Their

European history is one of explicit rejection by the British: the convict transportation system. Was it any wonder that where cricket was concerned they were determined to prove their mastery? But their philosophy isn't that English one of genteel playing up. Theirs was to win, at all costs. There was a sense that their cricketing prowess was an act of revenge. A tour there was inevitably bruising, and our record there was appalling. There was extra pressure this time around too.

We finally had a Black captain, Frank Worrell, who by this time was one of the elder statesmen of the team. It had taken a concerted campaign by C. L. R. James, who had returned to edit the *Nation* and campaigned for a Black captain all throughout the late fifties. This had come to a head on 30 January 1960, when Charran Singh was given run-out in a hugely controversial call. The crowd exploded and bottles were thrown. James wrote that this anger wasn't aimed solely, or even mainly, at the call but was instead partly down to anger around the ongoing issue of the captaincy. It was said that Learie Constantine went onto the field to try to placate the crowd and caught one of the bottles; he was an impeccable fielder even then.

By 1960 Worrell was the only one of the three Ws who remained. But he was ably assisted at the crease by, among others, the physically slight but immensely powerful Rohan Kanhai. Legend has it that England arranged their field with someone close to him, perhaps at silly mid-on, which is saying that you feel comfortable the batter isn't going to get hold of this one. Kanhai caught the eye of the fielder and said, 'You sure you want to stand there?' The fielder took one look in his eye and decided that no, he actually didn't want to stand there.

Alf Valentine and Sonny Ramadhin remained as bowlers, alongside Wes Hall, our blistering fast bowler. We also had a player who was on his way to entering the conversation for the best all-rounder of all time. Garfield 'Garry' Sobers. He had been born in Barbados in 1936. When he started playing at school, he was a left-arm slow bowler who was rumoured to never have been coached. He went on to play for the Police club in Barbados. He made his debut for Barbados at sixteen years old, for the West Indies at seventeen. All who saw him bowl were astonished by his precision of length and direction, which would have been remarkable at any age. At this point, Sobers decided to get better with the bat. Much like a painter learning through observation of the greats, he took what the batters he faced did, added some of his own flair, and reproduced it at bat. In 1955, by the time he was nineteen, due to an injury to the captain, Jeffrey Stollmeyer, he was opening against the visiting Australia, where he reached 43 in about a quarter of an hour at the crease before being caught out. He toured England in 1957 and was solid if unspectacular as both bowler and batsman.

But back home the following year he both scored his maiden Test century against Pakistan and went on to bat for a total of 365, scoring thirty-eight fours but no sixes. He scored another two centuries in the series. He went on to play for Radcliffe in Central Lancashire, the same club Worrell had played for with such distinction. And there, admiring the effectiveness of the faster bowlers, he taught himself how to become one. Stopping only to learn how to bowl left-handed googlies and chinamen on a tour of India and Pakistan, in January of 1960, he was at bat with Frank Worrell in Bridgetown for the first

Test of England's tour. Over the course of nine and a half hours at bat, in one of the most astonishing stands ever, he scored 226 and Worrell 197 for a total of 399, though the Test would be drawn.

So, though we had all been aware of the steep task that faced our boys, as they arrived in Brisbane and the series began, we certainly felt like we had the players to be in with a shot.

The first innings was an absolute blockbuster of aggressive attacking batting. The West Indies batted first and made 453, with Sobers's 132 the top score, but assisted by 50 from Wes Hall, 60 from Gerry Alexander and 65 each from Frank Worrell and Joe Solomon. But an astonishing 181 from Norm O'Neill saw Australia ahead by 52 runs at the end of the first innings.

There was to be no repeat of the West Indian first innings in their second. The Australian Alan Davidson, who had taken 5 for 135 in the first innings, then took 6 for 87, as the West Indies reached 259, leaving only the final pair, Wes Hall and Alf Valentine, to bat on the final day.

The morning session saw Hall and Valentine score 25 but, more importantly, eat into the time that Australia had. As Australia came in to bat, they had two sessions to score the 233 they needed to win. It was felt to be only a matter of time.

But Wes Hall was electric that first session. He had gone on the trip to England in 1957 but was out of sorts and his impact was best described as minor on the pitch. He had announced himself a year later against India and took a Test hat-trick the following year in Pakistan. What a sight he must have been, 6 foot 5 and powerfully built as he came thundering down his 30-yard run, the crucifix his mother bought him for luck swinging around his neck, like he was the very wrath of God himself. He always said that his speed came from the 7-mile walk to and from his school in Barbados. Legend had it that Muhammad Ali was impressed by his physique on a visit to Lord's in 1966, saying, 'If I had your stamina I'd fight three men a night – two rounds for the first one, another two rounds, and then seven!' Under the glare of his astonishing speed and power, Bobby Simpson, Neil Harvey and Norm O'Neill all wilted for a paltry return that morning.

As the final session began, I was sat, alone, in the office. You could hear the crowd were utterly electric. Almost immediately the Australians were 92 for 6; only Alan Davidson and Richie Benaud, the captain, at 7 and 8, recognised batters. The wind seemed to be blowing towards a West Indies win.

Benaud would later describe how he told Don Bradman he was determined to go for the win. He was certain that the West Indies would crack. But Worrell was utterly calm. And Benaud and Davidson were to put up 136 together. But as the session continued, what had once seemed like a gaping abyss of time to win, shrank and shrank and shrank. My feet were down from the table by now, my foot tapping to a manic beat.

And suddenly there was ten minutes of play and Australia needed nine runs to win. I was glad I was on my own at this point, as I was beyond words.

A Hall delivery. A shot to mid-wicket for a single. But then Davidson was run out after a call from Benaud he would later describe as terrible. I screeched as if I had stubbed my toe.

Out came Wally Grout the wicketkeeper (who would later

admit to being overcome with nerves and chain-smoking as he waited to enter the field), to stab at a couple of balls, more in a spirit of self-defence than anything else. Seven runs to win and four minutes to achieve them in. Could I imagine it, or did I hear others around the town shouting out? I stood wincing, waiting for the sound that would signal a thrashing four or six. Then a fierce Wes Hall delivery struck Grout in the centre of his chest and bounced agonisingly between fielders, allowing him to scutter along for a single.

Six to win. Seven balls.

A Hall bouncer that Benaud tried to hook but was caught behind by Alexander.

Five to win. Six balls.

Hall to Ian Meckiff, who gets a bye for a single off the second delivery he faces.

Four to win. Four balls.

Hall to Grout who, shaking from nicotine and nerves, swings and skies it. Four fielders are under it, they get in each other's way and it drops to the ground. Grout throws himself towards the crease, but he's run out.

Three to win. Three balls.

Hall to Meckiff, who pulls high into the outfield. A four! But it doesn't have the legs. They went for the three, but Conrad Hunte scoops it up with an 80-yard throw.

Scores level. Two balls.

Their number eleven, Lindsay Kline, the spin bowler, clipped his first ball to forward square-leg and set off for a run. But Solomon wasn't going to let that happen. He had grown up in what was then British Guiana, where legend had it that he would throw marbles at mangoes to hone his aim. The ball left his hand as sweet as any mango and hit the stumps side on. And that was Meckiff out.

'Hall will bowl to Kline ... and here's the single that will win the match for Australia ... he's out! He's run out! Oh, it's a tie!'

There it was. The first tie in Test history. So many hours of play and it all came down to the penultimate ball.

I sat down, exhausted. I wanted to find someone, to check that I had actually just heard what had happened. I could hear the crowd coming through the radio. It was left to me to try to find ways of putting all this into words. On the table my flask of coffee stood untouched. I had not needed it.

The ripples from that moment moved outwards over the coming days, months and years.

In February 1961 a crowd of hundreds of thousands of Australians waved the West Indies team goodbye. Australia had won the series 2–1. But it was clear who had won people's hearts. *Wisden* described how the visitors were 'given a send-off the like of which is normally reserved for Royalty and national heroes'.[8] It seemed to signal a potential future for the sport that captured the hearts of cricket fans around the world. There was a quality of joy in that West Indies team that transmitted itself to all who saw them. And there, at the centre, was the quiet, self-possessed Frank Worrell. To have a Black captain making the decisions at that moment, under that pressure, and to stand up to it and excel ... The great C. L. R. James wrote to him and said that if we could play well – not beat Australia, but play well – that would be the end of colonialism.

There had historically not been a coherent identity shared between the islands that made up the West Indies. Partly that was due to simple facts of geography: Jamaica is almost 1,200 miles from Trinidad, 1,300 miles from Barbados; Guyana lies almost 600 miles from Barbados. But any shared identity was exacerbated by their parallel and indeed often competing colonial histories. They were not so much nations as industrial hubs, often feeding resources to competing nation states. More than this, any sort of community between the enslaved was actively discouraged, as it could prove dangerous. There had been the successful Haitian Revolution at the end of the nineteenth century. Uprisings in Barbados in 1816, Demerara in 1823 and Jamaica in 1831–32 were brutally put down. Common cause between estates, never mind separate islands, was not to be encouraged.

A couple of years before the Australian tour, in 1958, the West Indies Federation had been founded, which was an attempt to form a federated political identity. The plan was for the islands to then achieve joint independence as one entity in a similar way to how Australia had in 1901. But it was riven with division and never really got going before it ended in 1962. I actually interviewed the first and only president of the federation, Grantley Adams. His first words were, 'Mac, what are we going to do about the cricket?'

But on that tour, in that play, in that moment – with that team facing the most pressure it was possible to face on a cricket pitch – there was Worrell. A Black man. A West Indian man. There couldn't be a more positive expression of aspiration. He was born on Barbados, and lived and worked on Trinidad and Jamaica. In 1947 he had moved from Barbados to Jamaica, which had been seen by some as a betrayal, but was in fact an early sign of his pan-island worldview. And it meant now that we could all share him. When he had called out, 'Good luck, Lindsay,' to the number eleven Australian batter in Brisbane, he had meant it. Frank always said that Lindsay's mouth had moved but no sound had come out.

When, later in the series, Worrell insisted Garry Sobers walk before the umpire's finger went up, he seemed the living embodiment of cricket's decency and fair play. From that point onwards, every West Indian player would do the same.

There had always been a stillness, a poise, a dignity to Worrell as a batsman. It was as if he had an extra allotment of time for every shot. It was said that he even ducked under a malevolent bouncer with elegance. He brought that stillness and dignity to the role of captain. When, in 1962, the Indian captain, Nari Contractor, was hit in the head and required several blood transfusions, the first man in the queue was Frank Worrell. He inspired his junior colleagues by his actions. He took an interest in them that went far beyond his teammates as cricketers. He had plotted out a path for Wes Hall in the English leagues and Australian state cricket. He'd found a job for him while he played for three years in Trinidad. Wes Hall would later say he 'deserved a Nobel prize' and made Worrell the best man at his wedding. He was the man that every player talked to, went to with any problem, whatever it was. His legacy was in the players whose lives he changed.

Wes Hall would go on to play as the visiting pro for Accrington for three summers. He told the story of a young boy shouting out: 'Mum, there's a Black man in the street.' Wes Hall explained that though Blackman was a common name in Barbados, his name was Wesley Hall and he was the new professional at the cricket club. Worrell had invited him to join him there and began a mentoring relationship that lasted for years. Wes Hall became a member of the Senate in Barbados and later minister for tourism and sport in the Barbados government. He was manager of the West Indies cricket team in 2001 and a selector, as well as president of the West Indies Cricket Board from 2001 to 2003. Hall was knighted in the Queen's birthday honours list for services to sport and the community.

I saw Frank Worrell several times in my twenties. He was so gracious, so considered. I was keen to draw him out and get some sense of him. But he repelled my novice questions with consummate grace and ease. He was famous for dozing off in the changing room while he was waiting to go out and bat. If your captain is so relaxed he's fallen asleep then you're likely to be more relaxed. I was so grateful that I got to know him. He would die tragically young of leukaemia in 1967. Thousands crowded to celebrate his life in Barbados. Thousands more at Westminster Abbey came to pay their respects – the first time a cricketer had ever been granted a memorial service there. In 2009 a then seventy-four-year-old Nari Contractor inaugurated the Sir Frank Worrell Memorial Blood Drive. It is celebrated as Sir Frank Worrell Day in the state of West Bengal.

In 2017 I received a call to give the Frank Worrall Memorial Lecture, which I was honoured and delighted to do. Everton Weekes was there, whom I had met when we had co-commentated on the cricket all those years before. We had a drink that night at the hotel. Everton was almost ninety by then. But his eyes were bright when he talked about Frank. He said that he and Frank had been very close: 'I'm still here because he always said he'd send for me when he needed me, so he clearly doesn't need me yet.' We spoke of Frank, as a player, as a captain and as a man. We talked of that day, in December 1960.

In his later years Wes Hall would tell the story of the moment he went to his captain for advice on how to bowl that iconic penultimate ball. Frank Worrell looked him calmly in the eye and said, 'Well, don't bowl a no-ball. Or you'll never be able to land in Barbados again.' That was it. But then Worrell called him back over and said, though he didn't have any special tactics or words of wisdom, the batsman didn't know that. So, if he moved the man at backwards square-leg two feet to the right and then two feet to the left, it would look like he and Hall had cooked up some brilliant plan. 'Let's see how they deal with that.' And it was that fielder, who had taken two steps right and then left – Solomon – who would win the match with his wonder throw. The ground erupted. In the centre of the maelstrom, the still centre of the world, Frank Worrall, the calmest man in the ground.

3

On Tour

West Indies Tour of England, 1963

'Could you please tell Mr Constantine that Trevor McDonald is here to see him?'

I sat down in the hotel lobby and tried forlornly to get warm. I can tell you that Britain is cold. You can think of the times in your life you've been cold. But as a child of the Caribbean, you really didn't know what cold was until you got there. And the colours are a different sort. In the tropics there is a vibrancy to things, a quality of the light. In Britain it felt as if there were browns and greens and greys. It felt damp even when it wasn't raining. It was May 1962, and I was wearing my heaviest suit and an overcoat but I was still cold. As I sat, I wondered what exactly I was going to say to him. The short answer was 'help' but I rather felt I needed to say more than that.

I had been sent to London by Radio Trinidad to report on the conference being held to discuss the date of Trinidadian independence and the formation of the constitution. There was, for obvious reasons, huge interest in the progress of this conference back home. Our diligent sales manager had even managed to get a lucrative sponsorship for these ten-minute bulletins. The only problem was that the official bulletins were thin gruel indeed. They would report, 'Delegates met today at Marlborough House and discussed matters of mutual interest. They have agreed to meet tomorrow morning.' I reasoned that it didn't matter how slowly I said that, it wasn't going to fill ten minutes. My attempts to get more information from delegates were met with an extremely straight bat. But I had one last plan. The legendary former cricketer Learie Constantine was present at the conference in his role as Trinidad and Tobago's High Commissioner, which he had begun the previous year. I knew him a very little at this point, having interviewed him a couple of times. But I didn't know if our relationship extended to my throwing myself upon his mercy.

Though he was winding down by the time my real interest in cricket was kindled, you couldn't help but know of his legend growing up in Trinidad. He was famed as the most perfect kind of instinctive player. Some seem to have learned strokes from a book but Learie played as if he was constantly improvising. Those who saw him said he played more like a jazz musician than anything else. He bowled with a deceptive pace. His fielding was electric: balls collected at full pace and thrown back like the snap of an elastic band. His joints seemed able to bend in ways other men's didn't. A ball that would be given up as a lost cause by any mere mortal was suddenly in his hand, propelled back towards the wicket with unerring aim. Though he was never captain, everyone knew he should have been. That injustice lit a fire in him that C. L. R. James would later characterise as 'the revolting contrast between his first-class status as a cricketer and his third-class status as a man'.[9] It was James who helped Learie see that there were horizons beyond cricket. How cricket revealed the way the world worked.

His father was the grandson of enslaved people, his mother the daughter of enslaved people. One of his earliest memories was of playing in the road when he was perhaps four or five and a cart came along. His mother shouted out that if he played in the road 'these white men would pass straight over him'. He has said that was the moment when he first realised that white men were indifferent to the lives of Black people. He got his first cricket bat when he was four, made from a branch of a coconut tree. The ball was a grapefruit dried in the sun, then, with the rind removed, it was possible to get 40 or 50 runs out of it before it fell apart. Learie's father had travelled to England in 1900. Learie was named after an Irish man his father had met who showed him such a good time in Ireland that he promised to name his son after him.

He came from a family of cricketers: both his father and uncle were first-class cricketers. His father, Lebrun, toured England with the West Indies and was the first West Indian to score a hundred there. Learie always said his mother was a good enough wicketkeeper to play first-class cricket. Though he was obsessed with cricket, Learie became a legal clerk. But there was a very firm ceiling on where that job would take him, with his skin colour. He toured England in 1923. The crowds wondered at this joyful, exuberant batsman. He'd had to give up his job as a legal clerk to tour England. So, for the next few years, he worked incredibly hard on his game. He made the decision to target the next tour in 1928. If he played well enough, he would try to become a professional cricketer.

His performances for the West Indies on tour in England in 1928 included a drive so fierce it broke the bowler Jack Hearne's finger and earned him a move to the cricket club in the tiny town of Nelson, Lancashire, in 1929. The only other Black man in town was the rag-and-bone man and at first children followed him down the street asking if he was a miner and whether he could wash it off with soap. To begin with there were letters sent that said, as he characterised it, 'that he couldn't play for toffee and should leave Nelson'. He recalls his heart being broken. But his wife said that they must fight. So, he stayed for nine years, won the Lancashire League championship seven times, was runner-up twice. The letters had stopped by then. The rumour went around that there had been an exam question at some point that asked the children in Nelson to say who Constantine the Great was. And one boy answered, 'He plays for Nelson.' He would play for ten years at Nelson, scoring 4,451 runs, taking 424 wicket catches in 119 games.

During the Second World War Learie worked as a Ministry of Labour welfare officer with the West Indian workers in the factories in the north-west. He had a clear sense of the hostile social conditions that many of them faced, but was an immensely popular figure from his cricketing days. His presence was often enough to calm situations. He told one story from the time about a dance hall. White workers living in a hostel had objected to Black workers staying in the same hostel. Learie's solution was a brilliant example of how he approached the role. He said he would stay in the hostel for a few weeks, so the workers could see what it was like living with a Black man. He had been staying there for a while when, one evening, there was a dance and a US serviceman, an officer, came all the way down the hall and said, 'We don't have Black men at dances.' Learie responded with anger and was walking down the hall ready to have a fight outside with the officer. But by the time he had walked the length of the hall, he realised what the downside would be to this: the news stories; the negative impact for the West Indian community more generally. Instead, he just let the bouncer shove the officer out of the dance and returned to it.

In 1943 Learie was thrown out of the Imperial Hotel in London. He was playing in a match at Lord's. He'd travelled with his wife and teenage daughter and had phoned ahead to say he'd like to book, and made sure they didn't have a problem with the fact he was Black. It was to be another twenty-odd years before Britain made racial discrimination illegal, so they could refuse him service legally. But the hotel said there would be no problem. The family arrived and were shown to their room. But almost immediately a porter came up and said, 'The manageress would like to speak to you.' She said, 'You can stay one night but no more. You're not welcome here.' It transpired that there were American officers staying at the hotel who had raised objections. Learie's daughter said, 'We are in the wrong place, Daddy. They don't want coloured people.' It was pointed out by his companions that Learie was a British subject and a civil servant. The manageress's reply was, 'He is a n*****.'

On this occasion, he decided enough was enough and took the hotel to court. It was still felt to be a lost cause: a Black man up against a white-owned hotel. There were questions asked in Parliament. When it was revealed that Learie had taken the hotel to court, one MP called out, 'I hope he bowls 'em out.' And he did. He won a landmark case in the history of racial discrimination.

This time, letters flooded in congratulating him for what he had done.

He was awarded the MBE in 1945. The following year Learie was elected by fellow players to lead the Dominions team that beat England at Lord's.

While playing he had qualified as a solicitor by correspondence course and was called to the bar in 1954, returning to Trinidad that year. Learie had wanted to contribute to the cause of nationalism and independence, but within a few months of his return he became hugely involved in the People's National Movement, along with Dr Eric Williams, previously a historian at Oxford. The political parties in Trinidad were set up to represent the interests of the different communities. Dr Eric Williams – it was always important that he be referred to as doctor; much was made of his PhD from Oxford: sometimes, at political rallies, he would quote Latin and the crowd would cheer – wrote a rather wonderful book called *Capitalism and Slavery*, which reframed the ending of slavery as an economic issue rather than a moral one. Eric was a Black Trinidadian. Upon independence, the opposition felt that they needed a leader with a PhD too, so they went and got Rudranath Capildeo, a doctor of philosophy from University College, London, to run against Williams. (It was felt that you must have great education to be a politician at that point. Woodford Square, where Williams held political meetings, was known as the University of Woodford Square. In many ways it was no surprise that the descendants of the enslaved so closely linked education and the opportunity to wield power. It was connected to my father's attitude towards education. Once you had it, it could not be taken away from you.)

But Constantine was one of the most famous Trinidadians in the land. He brought with him that visibility and broad popular support – and entered the government as minister of communications.

I was aware of the vast gulf between my own experiences as a young journalist still only in his early twenties and his. 'Trevor,' Learie said, holding out his hand and smiling, still a big man even in his sixties. At first our conversation was almost exclusively cricket. Gradually our talk turned to why I was in London, and my assignment, reporting on the conference. I explained my predicament and asked for his help. At first he said there was nothing he could do. He couldn't reveal anything from the day's conversations. But, after further entreaties, he said he would try to give some of the flavour of the day. And that was how it began.

We would meet at his hotel at the end of each day; I would ask my inane questions and he would answer them as best he could. Then I would do my broadcast. My only competitor was a gentleman working as a reporter for one of the Trinidadian papers, who could only phone his copy back in time for the following morning's edition, whereas I was on that evening. I remember the stringer being very suspicious of where I was getting my information from. It never, however, amounted to anything big – perhaps my biggest scoop was that they were planning to send for a specific constitutional lawyer from Trinidad. Learie made sure that he was giving nothing away that could cause any real problems, but he was able to give just enough of a sense of what was going on each day for me to build a report upon it.

I was too busy to do anything but work and certainly couldn't sightsee, but one day, sick of a press officer stonewalling me, I told him I was going to go to Epsom for the Derby that day. And he said that sounded like a much more interesting way to spend the day. Radio Trinidad were delighted, as it meant as well as my bulletin on the conference, they could include a report on what was an astonishingly popular event back home. And so I went to watch the Derby. It was carnage. Seven of the twenty-six runners fell or were brought down, including the race favourite. One of the horses broke its leg and had to be put down. Six jockeys had to go to hospital. That night, I did both my report on the conference and a report on the Derby. The next day, I saw the press officer, who just looked at me and said, 'Well, you're a good luck charm, aren't you.'

I received a delighted-sounding message from our head of sales that advertising revenue had never been higher. There was a Rediffusion office in Regent Street and I had been told to pay my respects to Lord Buckhurst, the man in charge. But on every one of my trips he hadn't been there. However, on the penultimate day, as I got out of a taxi, there he was waiting to get into it. I introduced myself. 'This chap Williams,' he said. 'Seems like a good sort. Seems like he'll get in. Do make sure what you say about him is the right sort of thing.' And with that he was off.

At the end of the conference, there was a drinks party at the hotel where the delegates were staying. Dr Eric Williams, soon to be prime minister of Trinidad and Tobago, was there. He was a serious, intense man and we were all a little scared of him. At one point he turned to me: 'Ah, Trevor McDonald, you're the one sending those bulletins home. What have you been putting in them?' I was keen to protect my source, so I simply said, 'Not very much.' He replied, 'That's not what my brother in Trinidad tells me. He says everyone is glued to their wireless each night.' I think I smiled weakly at that.

I thanked Learie Constantine profusely and returned to Trinidad. And that was the real beginning of my career as a journalist. My reports had not gone unnoticed. I was felt to be a safe pair of hands and gradually I became the natural choice for the bigger interviews.

The following year, 1963, I sat enthralled by my wireless as the West Indies toured England with a newly won appreciation for what the commentator meant when he described a morning as 'chilly'. It was Frank Worrell's last tour as captain and it was a fitting tribute. Every single Test match sounded as full of West Indies fans as English. They certainly made the majority of the noise. In front of these fans the team put on a brilliant display. From the first moment, they seemed to have a sense of harmony as a team that felt special. Partly it was because the UK was no longer a shock to the system as it had been for so many previous teams. They were able to deal with the rain as previous teams perhaps would not have been. Nine of the team had played in England. We had genuine pace in our bowlers with Wes Hall, Charlie Griffith and Lester King, the now familiar spin of Valentine, plus Lance Gibbs and Willie Rodriguez, the leg-spinner. Not forgetting the remarkable players that were Garry Sobers and Worrell himself.

Sobers gave an astonishing display. He was dominant in every way a cricketer could be. I remember one six off the very good English fast bowler Brian Statham during the first Test at Old Trafford that was picked off with the insouciance of someone swatting a pesky fly. And when England were attempting a fightback, who was it who bowled a googly that was gloved to Worrell in the slips? Sobers. It seemed to me as if he was saying that whichever way England wanted to play, brains or brawn, he was the better man.

West Indies won the match by 10 wickets, Sobers taking 4 of them. Over the tour he made 322 runs, took 20 wickets and made 29 catches. The West Indies won the series 3–1.

Though he had a knee that was troubling him, Rohan Kanhai managed to make the half-centuries where they mattered. As ever, his knack for timing the hit felt almost magical. He had an array of shots that seemed to almost trouble the commentators for how to describe them. He was advised by a doctor to miss the final Test at the Oval, as he needed an immediate operation to fix his knee. Instead he played and hit 30 and 77 as the West Indies won.

Wes Hall and Charlie Griffith began a partnership that would define the next few years of West Indian cricket. Hall, especially, seemed at times to be auditioning as a Greek god, bowling at top speed for hour upon hour. Hall bowled 40 overs in the final innings of the second Test at Lord's because he knew the team needed him to.

But there was to be an event that would complicate my feelings of simple pride in that series.

Learie Constantine was watching the West Indies play Gloucester on tour in Bristol on 4 May 1963 when he was informed about a bus boycott organised by Bristol's Black community in response to the Bristol Omnibus Company's decision not to employ Black people, as compelled by the union. By the time he arrived it had been going on for several months. Over the coming months Learie became involved. He spoke to the union leaders. He wrote articles in the press. I never had the sense from talking to him that he enjoyed the day-to-day processes of politics. He liked good causes and he wanted to do whatever he could to improve the lot of the common man, but he saw it as a means to an end, rather than being a devout politician. He didn't have a broader political ideology. He had always believed that people should treat each other with common decency. There had, however, been a gradual sharpening of his views on racial discrimination. His reaction wasn't typically anger, but to try to find common cause. He met injustice with compassion and good humour at every stage. But, as he'd shown all those years before with the hotel, he wasn't afraid to hold a line of principle. And here, in Bristol, he found one. The Foreign Office felt strongly that this wasn't a proper thing for a high commissioner to be doing. His own government sided with the Foreign Office. I remember finding that extraordinary. It was big news at home, and I remember reporting on it. Eric Williams pushed him out into the cold and he never forgave him for that. He felt he used him when he needed him then kicked him out when it was politically expedient. He would have hated that. It may have been how politics functioned, but it wasn't cricket. His intervention assisted in a speedy resolution of the dispute, but he left his role as high commissioner in 1964.

But in Britain he appeared on early editions of *Question Time*. He became rector of the University of St Andrews and a governor of the BBC. In 1969 he was made a baron: the first ever Black peer in the House of Lords. But he was in poor health and by this point was really too ill to participate. It was a huge shame that he wasn't able to be there at full strength. We were raised to have huge respect for Parliament. I know the pride he would have felt at that.

He was told by doctors that he needed to leave London for a warmer climate for the sake of his lungs. But he refused to. He died in 1971 and was posthumously awarded Trinidad and Tobago's highest honour, the Trinity Cross – the first sportsperson ever to receive it.

For some, it was too late. The damage had been done.

I met him a few times over the years and was saddened by his mistreatment, which I don't think he ever really forgave. He was a journalist, a lawyer, a politician and a civil rights activist – but he was always a cricketer.

I think that, as time went on, perhaps he wasn't as robust on race as people like their politicians to be. He was in many ways shy and retiring, full of quiet dignity. He became slightly out of step with a harder, less-forgiving attitude towards racial discrimination. His decision to view the racial discrimination without bitterness may have appeared to some as apologism or acceptance. But he was one of the most admirable men I've ever met. It certainly wasn't conscious, but I have to admit that I made my way through life on similar principles.

I remember the story of Learie, in 1929, and the South African all-rounder Jimmy Blanckenberg, who was rumoured to have told the Jamaican batsman George Headley, 'Where I come from, we don't fraternise with you fellows.' Constantine had replaced Blanckenberg as the professional at Nelson and went to shake his hand before the match. Blanckenberg turned his back on him. Constantine bowled fast and short and Blanckenberg finished the match covered in bruises.

All of those who followed Learie are grateful to him. Me especially.

4

The Bushmen

India Tour of the West Indies, 1971

'*Howzaaaaaaat!*'

I'd nicked it, I knew I had, and been caught at leg slip. I began to walk before the umpire reacted. 'Bad luck, Trevor!' called one of my sympathetic teammates. 'I told you,' I mumbled, to myself as much as anyone else, 'I'm really not a very good leg-side player.'

It was a glorious summer's day in 1970 and I had made my first contribution to the long history of the Bushmen. A three. The first team from Bush House had been led out by Hugh Carleton Greene in June 1942, legend maintaining that that inaugural game was interrupted by news that Rommel had taken Tobruk.

Though I was disappointed by my performance, I couldn't have been happier to be there. It is hard to communicate what it meant to someone like me, to not only be in England, playing cricket on a sun-dappled village green, but for the team I was playing for to be connected to Bush House. It was from there that so many of the voices I had grown up listening to emanated. And now my voice was one of them.

From my first trip to Britain, when I had been so indebted to Learie Constantine, I had kept up those contacts I had made, including some at the BBC. At Radio Trinidad we took a lot of BBC World Service feeds – if an event was big enough, there was no point us trying to report on it. When John Kennedy was shot I was on duty; we went on for some minutes and then we switched to the World Service as they were better able to cover the story. And, of course, people from London often came out to places like Trinidad to see their customers. In fact, I imagine it was quite a plum job. So, the BBC World Service people would come out and I would take them out and impress upon them, with stultifying regularity, how much I wanted to come and work in London and that they should let me know if an opportunity ever arose for me to apply for a role. I also went back to London on a broadcasting scholarship to spend some time at the BBC. I took courses in how to do interviews and read the news and chase down stories. I bored everyone rigid again telling them I wanted a job in England. The World Service were very keen to keep the Caribbean service refreshed with those who had recently been in the Caribbean, so that the programming was in some way up to date.

I had left Radio Trinidad for a couple of years, as I needed money to get married. I had worked for the British High Commission, who wanted someone to give them good commercial advice about local matters. I was a commercial officer there. I cannot say it was where my passion lay, but I did it for economic reasons. I then did some freelance work for the newly arrived television. I read the news and I presented a discussion programme called *Dialogue*. And then, one day in 1969, Christopher Bell, the assistant head of the Overseas Regional Service, called me up and said there was a vacancy for a producer at Bush House for the Caribbean. Would I like to come? It was a stroke of immense good fortune. Who gets invited to come to London for a job? I felt that it was probably a good idea not to just scream 'yes', and that I should ask some questions, to look like a serious person. But the only question I could think of was, 'What would happen to my books?' To which they replied that they would ship them over as part of their offer.

So, over the coming weeks, I made all of the arrangements. In a series of tearful dinners I said goodbye to my siblings and parents, who responded with those equal parts sadness, pride and bemusement that is an island parent's lot. A cousin of a friend of a neighbour owned a house in Guildford, so it was decided I should rent that. I knew nothing about Guildford other than the fact it was in the fine cricketing county of Surrey, and less than an hour away from Bush House. I arrived on the by now well-trodden path from the Caribbean to London.

I was, of course, always aware that as a West Indian man I was in a minority. I have always been asked if racism manifested in my day-to-day life. Of course, I understand the question. So many were affected. I am not ignorant of my context. The Race Relations Act had only been brought into force in 1965: before that it was not illegal to refuse goods or services to someone on the basis of their race. The National Front had been formed in 1967, only two years before I arrived. Their membership increased rapidly over the next five years. The year that I arrived, NF candidates were fielded in local elections and some of them picked up as much as 10 per cent of the vote. Enoch Powell had given his 'Rivers of Blood' speech in 1968. There was a well-documented and undeniable tension seething on the streets of Britain. There had been large-scale racist attacks in Liverpool in 1948 and Notting Hill in 1958, not to mention the murder of individuals. Nobody could be unaware of the racism that West Indians faced in Britain. Powell's use of the phrase 'whip hand', in the context of people for whom the whip was wielded over their great-grandparents, was as grotesque a use of language as I can conceive of.

I have racked my brains for evidence of this in my own life. I'm not sure if it was my concentrating on paying my mortgage or my unconsciously repeating my father's worldview. I was not unaware of the harsh treatment others received, but I can honestly say that I did not experience this first hand. I can only come to the conclusion that I was, again, lucky. For one I was ensconced in the United Nations that was Bush House. Though there weren't many Black broadcasters in the country, in Bush House you would sit in the canteen with people from Tanzania, or Russian specialists. From time to time, walking down Aldwych, I would be reminded that my bubble was certainly not the nation. There was perhaps a second glance, a widening of the eyes. But the work was all-consuming. Or, at least, I let it consume me – perhaps as a way of burying any sadness I felt about being away from my family, I was utterly focused on making the best of my very good fortune and determined not to be found wanting. The

World Service – or the BBC Empire Service, as it had been known until 1965 – had a Christmas messages show every year, where people in the UK could send messages back to their families. Mostly it was, 'Hello, Mum, it's cold here, hope I see you soon'-type stuff. I remember neighbours would go to people's houses to listen to the Christmas messages. And if someone from our village, or even the island, was mentioned it would be a moment of real excitement. So I knew what was at stake. We were a conduit between those halfway around the world and home. It was a big deal. I remembered with fondness that patrician tone of the World Service. That things are under control. That the BBC is talking to the entire world. The BBC Empire Service had begun broadcasting in December 1932: an English-language service, at that time squarely aimed at what George V described in his very first Christmas message as 'men and women, so cut off by the snow, the desert, or the sea, that only voices out of the air can reach them'. Lord Reith, the first director-general of the BBC, had always been passionate about the role that broadcasting could play in forging a sense of unity, though it was not one that politicians often recognised.

It was the war that saw the BBC first broadcast to the world in languages other than English. The huge propaganda value these broadcasts could have was understood. There was a constant tussle between those who wanted this service to be the mouthpiece of the Foreign Office and those who wanted full independence. The BBC's broadcasts during the Second World War won it tremendous trust throughout the world. And the World Service had a tremendous trust and authority, perhaps as a legacy of that.

Counter-intuitively, West Indian politicians, who had tended to be very difficult to get hold of in the West Indies, were now available to me. They would present themselves for an interview at Bush House because they knew it would go all around the islands. We would get to see them all. The World Service unlocked doors. One morning I was invited to interview Winifred Atwell, the great Trinidadian pianist, and she offered me bourbon. I had never had it before, but managed to drink it down. We raised a glass to Frank Worrell, who had died from leukaemia a couple of years before at the age of forty-two, when Barbados had been an independent nation for four months.

Within a few months of being at Bush House I was approached in the corridor and asked if I played cricket. My honest answer – not for a few years now, but religiously before that – was seen to be good enough. I hadn't actually played that much even in secondary school because football had been played more at our school. I shouted so much for my school team that I couldn't speak in class the next day. And, once I'd started my job at Radio Trinidad, watching it and listening to cricket? Yes, obsessively. But actually standing at the crease? Very rarely.

I worried a little that the Bushmen thought I might be some sort of secret weapon. Technically, I was an all-rounder as I was equally lacking in any real proficiency with both ball and bat. But I turned up for a practice session and realised that I was not going to be drastically sub-par. Indeed, I settled into my role batting at 5 or 6 – regularly troubling double figures, but not that often beyond – and delivering the odd medium-paced, medium-length delivery, which, every now and then, deceived a batsman. But there is a kind of magic about playing cricket – in its rhythms, its language; in the things that did not need to be said between us because we just knew they needed to happen. That feeling of lumbering over to chase a ball and tossing it back: that all was right with the world. This was an unconscious antidote to homesickness. Although not many of my teammates had grown up with a tree branch for a bat, or tennis balls dipped in water, it was the same game. It was the same language that we were able to speak together.

Now I look back, I am not unaware of the irony that I, a child of Trinidad, took cricket with me to England as a little parcel of home. Over the years, I would travel about the country, seeing parts of Britain I would never have seen otherwise. Most of the time I drove, but sometimes the team would take the train together, and these journeys became a kind of test of one's stamina. I remember once we went to Eastbourne to play the England Women's Team. I played against Rachael Heyhoe Flint, the former captain. We were beaten out of sight. We would have been beaten anyway, but it didn't help that on the way there, it seemed as if at every stop, Jack de Manio, an early presenter of the *Today* programme, produced another bottle of gin from somewhere. By the time we arrived at Eastbourne the very short walk to the cricket ground felt like a very long one indeed, as we wobbled over there. We would play cricket and then go back to the bar of a local pub. The owner would say, 'I'm tired, but you take what you want and tell me.' And he left us to tot up what we'd drunk. We once went to play at a ground in Marlow, where T. S. Eliot lived. We played at Motspur Park too, a wonderful ground.

I was invited to play with other teams from time to time. I remember once playing for Baron John Hatch. I was fielding too close at cover and there was a huge guy and a spin bowler at the other end. Well, the spin bowler landed the ball exactly right (for him) and this huge guy got hold of it and . . . you just know when someone connects in a certain way. I remember thinking that I did not want to let any part of my body connect with that ball, so I ducked away. Hatch was furious. A tough Yorkshireman: 'Why did you do that?!' I was severely reprimanded for not catching him out. Another time we played against workers from HMP Parkhurst on the Isle of Wight. We were told to be careful how aggressively we appealed to certain people, as they were warders.

And then there were the various associated drinks and dinners. I got to know people in a way I would not have done without cricket. From the outside, I know that the social element of cricket can look exclusionary: too redolent of the old school tie; the wives in the clubhouse making sandwiches while the men swirl brandy and toast the King. One evening we played, and the local proprietors connected somehow to Hugh Carleton Greene. We were told there were drinks in the pub. But there was nobody present from the team we'd played. 'Oh no, we don't invite them, just our side.' So I went down to the pub where the other team were. They were the employees of the big houses. I couldn't have any truck with that sort of below-stairs stuff. The point of playing cricket is to respect the team you are playing. I don't think it was deliberately cruel, but it felt impolite to me not to drink with the opposing team. It had been drummed into us when we were young: do everything within the rules you can to win – but when the game is over, shake hands, go for a drink.

My world was my rented house in Guildford, Bush House, and the cricket pitches the Bushmen travelled to. But Bush House was a world unto itself. The entire building was abuzz with discussions around global politics – in the corridors, at our desks and in the bars. The canteen felt more like a university symposium. It was there that my feelings around what journalism was and should be were formed, watching how a story was probed and tested, in search of the truth. It was not, as has come to be the role of the media, our job to display the white heat of conflict around an issue, but to let it cool and find the core.

I once produced a story about Ghana's economy. A few weeks later our office received a letter from Ghana's economics minister, who said he'd missed the show and would greatly appreciate a copy of the broadcast. I showed this to my editor and said, 'I assume we shouldn't send this as he knows more than us about the economy of Ghana?' But he said, 'No, this happens from time to time,' and that he'd be interested in what we said. Bush House was full of great minds. There was a Russian expert known as Anatoly Goldberg. He was a prominent broadcaster who talked a lot about dissidents such as Joseph Brodsky and Aleksandr Solzhenitsyn. A few years later, when Solzhenitsyn was released, Goldberg went to the press conference and asked a question. And Solzhenitsyn said, 'Ah, Mr Goldberg, we meet at last.' He had heard his broadcasts. We were aware that what we did went out into the world and had a real impact. It was, in every sense of the words, a world service.

There was a minor tension early on because I was technically a producer but I desperately wanted to carry out the interviews. So I suggested that I do so to my boss. And, gradually, they allowed me to do this. The resistance from up the hierarchy stopped at some point and I was able to become more involved in that side of things. I reported on the Commonwealth Games in Edinburgh in 1970 and have golden memories of that summer watching Kenyan middle-distance runners and Jamaican sprinters.

The first time I went back to Trinidad after I'd moved away, my father and I sat on the balcony of his house and he would call out as everyone came past, 'My son has come home!' And when we went to the rum shop, for him to show me off, he would call out, 'My son has come from London to buy you all a drink!' Which, to be honest, had not been my plan, but was not something I felt able to countermand. He sat and watched, smiling, as they raised a glass. I would get little clues that they, or someone they knew, had listened to something I had been involved in. Selfishly, I was glad that what I worked on was something that we had all listened to, something that had been such a part of our lives. I hoped that there was some small sense that the struggle had been worth it in some way.

In January of 1971 I have to confess to almost entirely missing something that would come to seem of great import in later years. A slightly bad-tempered tour of Australia by England, remarkable for the adrenaline-dampening quality of the first two Tests, had reached Melbourne with some commentators worried there was a danger it would put spectators off the entire sport of cricket. But the weather saw that the third Test was abandoned after the third day. With a huge gap in their finances, both sides scheduled a seventh Test, but financial negotiations dragged on. And so I wasn't even aware of the match hastily scheduled for what would have been the fifth day of the Test. However, I read an article by Johnny Woodcock in the *Times* detailing how the fixture had been billed an England XI versus Australian XI, with the tobacco company Rothmans rustled up as an eleventh-hour sponsor. How they'd been expecting something like twenty thousand and instead got more than forty-six thousand for the first one-day international. Don Bradman may have told his team they were part of history. He said that the crowd had gone home happy enough that it would become a regular fixture in the cricketing calendar. But it felt more like an oddity – terrible weather leading to crowds desperate for any cricket – a foot-note in the history of the game, than anything else. *Wisden* didn't even carry a report. But, as would later become clear, an Australian media magnate by the name of Kerry Packer certainly was paying attention.

I, however, had bigger fish to fry. India were on tour in the West Indies. I remember sitting in my front room in April 1971 and listening, first with horror and then a mounting sense of wonder, as the great Indian batsman Sunil Gavaskar announced himself to the world with a remarkable double century in the final Test at Queen's Park Oval. I had to admit I was rather glad not to be there. It was a timely reminder that no team is invincible. Although over the last few years it might have felt like we were. Garry Sobers had succeeded Frank Worrell as captain for Australia's tour of the islands, which we'd won 2–1, beating Australia for the first time. He'd been acclaimed as 'King Cricket' on the tour of England in

1966 (though perhaps those events were overshadowed by those later that year on the football pitch). He'd scored 722 runs, made 3 centuries, taken 20 wickets and 10 catches.

But then we were then beaten at home by England, which was a shock. And at the heart of it was a curious decision that Sobers made that was to echo on through history.

West Indies were 92 for 2, 215 runs ahead in the fourth Test, and everything looked set for a draw, when Sobers declared, going for the win. At the time, his thinking was not entirely unsound. This was an England team not well known for swift scoring – 215 to win in just under three hours looked a tall order. However, Sobers demonstrating his belief that they couldn't score at the required rate seemed to sting them into action, and they made the total with three balls to spare. The West Indies lost the Test and the series. That night, it was reported that an effigy of Sobers was hanged and burned in Port of Spain. It was an extremely febrile atmosphere. On the fifth day of the second Test at Sabina Park, Kingston, the police had released tear gas after a riot, and surreally the English vice-captain, Fred Titmus, lost four toes in a speed-boating accident.

What was strange was that, as a player, Sobers had still done well. He averaged more runs than any other player, was the West Indies second best for wickets, and best for catches. Later, he would write that he made the declaration because England's slow pace in every element of the game was boring him. They had bowled 22 overs in two hours. 'I wanted to make a game of it rather than letting the game die,' Sobers said. 'When things pay off you are great, and when they don't you are a darn idiot.'[10] Perhaps the problem was that he had succeeded Worrell, someone who, as a captain, was defined by his serene calm. And this decision came to be seen as the antithesis of that. It seemed to hark back to the days when opponents could bet on the West Indies cracking under the pressure.

Sobers's club form was just fine. In fact, in August 1968 he had become the first player ever to hit six sixes in one over, when he'd captained Nottinghamshire against Glamorgan in Swansea. Sobers had been after quick runs and a declaration when he faced the medium-pacer Malcolm Nash. Nash would later say his strategy was to keep pitching it to him and hope he whacked it up in the air. He certainly did. The first ball was clobbered over long-on for a big six. The second disappeared over the deep square-leg fence. The third cracked straight down the ground. The fourth ball was hammered over square-leg, and by this time the fielders were all making their way out towards the boundaries. With the fifth, Sobers cracked it out to long-off, where the fielder took the catch but was off balance and sat down on the boundary rope. There were shouts of both 'six' and 'out' and Sobers who, after all, had been captained by Frank Worrell, had already begun to walk before the umpire called it a six. The sixth ball was hit so hard over mid-wicket that it left the ground and came to rest at a bus stop where a young boy found it and took it home. The fact that Sobers had once famously said hitting sixes didn't interest him just made it more memorable. He was that same blend of sinew and muscle as Worrell: liquid power. Off back foot and front, the bat moving so fast you could hardly see it. There has arguably never been a better hooker in the entire history of the game. The ball didn't loop up; it stayed flat, or went over the boundary at shin height. So though nobody could accuse him of failing as a player, it felt as if the team had lost its way with him as captain. We lost on tour in Australia and then drew in New Zealand.

But in April 1971, as the final draw confirmed that India had won the series 1–0, I sat listening to the commentators acclaim this cricketing nation for coming of age, celebrating their brilliant young batting talisman who seemed to toy with the bowlers. It would later transpire that Gavaskar had played through a terrible toothache, but refused to see the dentist in case the anaesthesia made him drowsy. When he made his double hundred, after spending a nail-biting half an hour in the 190s, the pitch had been invaded and he was lifted above their shoulders.

I heard the sound of the West Indian crowd, through the radio, so far away. And I realised, perhaps for the first time, really, that I would spend the next part of my life away from home, listening to it from a distance, the reverse of the first thirty years of my life.

5

Shots

West Indies Defeat England, 1973

'What a shot!'

The tennis ball smacked off my bat, a perfect flashing drive. It was as if Learie Constantine, Frank Worrell and Garry Sobers had all possessed me at once for a split second. With baited breath we watched as it sped deep mid-wicket towards the edge of the rooftop that marked our boundary, then groaned as it took an odd bounce and flipped up over the edge. We all knew what that meant. It would end up in the beer garden of the pub next door. It meant I would have to trudge downstairs, find the particularly truculent Belfast landlord and, with the same cowed shame of every young cricketer ever, ask for our ball back.

It was 1973 and we were on the roof of Ulster Television Studios. A group of us, with me as the chief instigator, had taken to playing cricket up there, partly to relieve the stress – but also because up there you could see the smoke from explosions. We'd work out with a local journalist where the plume was, then go downstairs and tell our colleagues where the bombs had gone off. I was not a natural war reporter – my natural caution shading into what I deemed genuine cowardice. Often, I would tell my colleagues I was going next door to use the phone and then sit under the desk until I had stopped shaking. I wasn't quite sure what the symbolism of us playing the quintessentially English colonial sport might be, so wasn't delighted by the idea of advertising it to an entire pub. I wondered, yet again, if leaving the gentility of Bush House had been the right decision.

However, after three years in Aldwych, I had started to wonder if perhaps there was more that I wanted to accomplish, or at least attempt. I could see how you might spend your whole career in Bush House, immersed in gold-standard journalism. But there was a soporific quality to that thought. And I was determined to keep pushing myself. I was also more and more curious about television. I had already done some back in Trinidad and had enjoyed it. I knew it was a huge step up to the standards at the BBC, but I certainly wanted to at least try my hand. I think at some point, early on, I'd even done a screen test to see if I might work as a presenter on television, only to be told that I had done fine but had a mediocre voice. Which I nodded along to. Sounded about right.

So I thought all my Christmases had come at once when one day I was in my office and the telephone rang and a voice at the other end said, 'Trevor McDonald? We'd like to talk to you about television.' And a few days later, I arrived and there was wine and smoked-salmon sandwiches. And we began to talk about what me trying out for a role on BBC television might look like. I tried to remain calm, but inside I was jubilant. But then he said, 'You see, we've been having calls with the Race Relations Board and they say we must have more Black people on the news.' I took a big gulp of wine and nodded politely, but from that point in the conversation onwards I was determined that that shouldn't be the framework for my next career step. A week later I called them back and politely turned down the offer.

I can't say why, rationally, other than it didn't feel like how I wanted to make my way through the next part of my career. I had no issue with the Race Relations Board, or with the BBC coming to that decision. I thought there should be more (or certainly at least some) Black people on the BBC. But I didn't want to be that person, getting the role with exclusively that reasoning. I wanted to get ahead because of what I did, not because of who I was. Perhaps it was something I had absorbed from my father, my version of taking the boys from the big house fishing in our river. I was not so naive as to not see race. I saw it, but I chose not to make it central to myself as a journalist. I am aware how, for many, concentrating on the next rung ahead of you can so easily become pulling the ladder up behind you.

It was only a couple of months later that I took the step that was to change my life for ever. After the fourth drink in the bar on a Friday evening, I used to bore my Bush House friends by telling them how I had once done television in Trinidad. They got quite fed up with this and, after a while, they said, 'If you think you're so good, why don't you go to ITN? They've got jobs there constantly at the moment.' And I stopped talking for a little while. ITN had been founded in 1955 and right from the beginning had seen itself as in competition with the BBC. They were the first to broadcast from the front lines, the first to interview people on the street, and they'd had the first female newsreader. Their coverage of enormous events like the moon landing and general elections consistently outperformed the BBC. They had an energy in their attitude towards news. Not least of all they seemed to believe that people genuinely wanted this approach to the news and could be engaged by it. But, in many ways, my initial application was driven by a mildly petulant desire to show my BBC friends what was what. So, I went for an interview. I brought a short novel along because I assumed I would be waiting for ages. But, in the end, I'd only read two pages before I was called in. And the interview, from my point of view at least, went not unfavourably. From my long conversation with colleagues in the canteen and bars of Bush House, I had a pretty decent working knowledge of the current geopolitical hotspots. I also had a genuine passion for communicating global events to the most people possible. I spoke about how listening to the radio had helped me understand how a world was waiting out there. And, after a while, somebody called me up from ITN and said, 'Would you like to come back and have another chat with us?' The second time it was less formal, and with another more senior figure present, which I took to be a good sign. And then the next day they offered me the job. I was enormously flattered, but asked for some time to think about it.

'You said *what*?!' was my friend's response when I told him in the bar in Bush House. 'Why didn't you say yes immediately?' The answer, I suppose, was that I was in no way unhappy at the BBC. I had my job, which I enjoyed. I had the cricket team and my friends. But the more I thought about it, the more I thought that the only thing holding me back was fear of the unknown. So I decided to make the move to ITN.

I had been scrupulously clear in all of the conversations that I was absolutely not joining as their 'Black reporter', with a beat consisting of Brixton, Tottenham, Notting Hill and Birmingham. I wanted to cover the biggest stories there were, wherever they were. And at that point the very biggest story was Northern Ireland. So off I went almost immediately upon joining.

I found myself staying at the Europa Hotel in Belfast, which seemed always to be followed by the descriptor 'the most bombed hotel in the world'. I couldn't help but feel that wasn't somewhere I wanted to stay. From time to time when you were staying there the IRA would phone through and say they'd planted a bomb, and then everyone would trudge outside and stand and wait for the all-clear. I have never taken quicker showers in my life, as I was fixated on the idea that the call would come and I'd be led outside to wait shivering in a bathrobe.

The first time I was near an explosion and experienced the animal fear of running the other way, that metal taste of fear in a crowd that is panicking, I remember lying flat on my stomach in a rundown Belfast housing estate, trying to work out which direction gunfire was coming from and how far away it was. There was such bitterness and anger around you all the time. Earlier that day I'd covered one of the regular riots and witnessed paving stones ripped up and thrown at a police station. I watched with astonishment as an elderly man explained, like Socrates to his students, how to break down the paving stones but keep their sharp edges, so as to cause maximum damage. His voice was calm, his tone without rancour. It was just one of those tasks that must be accomplished. Our eyes met, and he smiled in an almost bashful way. In an effort to escape the soldiers charging in to break up the riot, we ran into an open doorway gratefully. There I sat and drank tea with a woman who had been born in Trinidad.

I remember one evening going to a house where a masked gunman had burst in and opened fire, killing three people. The house was trailed with blood: on the floor, the bannisters, the kitchen and pooled on the living-room carpet. I was interviewing someone who was telling me what had happened and a young girl of perhaps eight or nine ran in and corrected them: the gunman had run left, not right. As we left, I saw her with her sister, and it hit me that those children had seen what had happened, would carry that with them their whole lives. And that every time something like that happened it created children with the purest motive of revenge. There's no surer way of creating mothers who will raise children to hate than murdering their parents in front of them.

You quickly saw how deeply enmeshed in violence these communities were. A reification of an eye for an eye, and the whole world blind. I had thought, perhaps naively, that being there, talking to people on every side, I would come to some sort of greater understanding of what was happening, and perhaps even the potential solutions. But I'm not sure I ever did. You would come up against the idea that the communities were just so different that they couldn't mix. Once, I was interviewing a senior Unionist leader and I asked him, when it came down to it, what the biggest difference was, culturally, between Catholic and Protestant. He thought for a moment and said, 'Do you know – well, you know – the Catholics have different ways of living, and they have many more children than we have, and so on.'

I said to him, 'You know, Minister, I think you have to come up with a better explanation than that.' I had never understood what the tension around marching was until I went and saw it. I would think, 'Why don't you march somewhere else?' It was only when you saw the tone of the marches – the provocative wish to march through each other's districts – that you saw how deeply embedded the provocation was. I march because you marched, so you march because I marched. And on and on, *ad infinitum*. It was impossible not to process what was happening there in some ways as part of a colonial story. I remember once speaking to a leading Protestant politician and asking why there were so few Catholic policeman. He started to tell me that because of their larger families, Catholics didn't make the physical requirements to be a police officer. I raised an eyebrow and suggested to him that a Black West Indian recognised discrimination when he heard it.

I once stumbled into a conversation about 'mixed communities' while being not quite up to speed with that phrase in the Irish context and, as my wife at that time was white, I said, 'Well, I have a mixed marriage.' 'Ah,' he said. 'Is your wife Catholic?' To them, it was religious difference that was at the centre of the universe, not race. And because it was the centre of their universe it powered this constant violence. Gunmen would open fire in bars crowded with people, others would plant bombs in busy shopping areas.

I covered a story about a group of Northern Irish children,

some Catholic and some Protestant, who were taken to England to spend time together. They reported being surprised at how well they got on. The majority of them had never spent time with someone of a different religion. The effort that you must expend on sectarianism: you must have to keep putting more and more energy into it. Because what tends to happen is that human beings find a way. If left to their own devices, they meet, talk, fall in love, get married, have children. And this is the antidote to the poison of sectarianism. So the system has to try to catch the children, radicalise them, try to make it so they never meet those on the other side of the divide. It has to function not through logic but as a kind of catechism.

I once stood in a cathedral in Dublin and watched, moved to tears, as the caskets were carried in procession from the victims of a series of massive explosions. Some of them were children's coffins. Some of them clearly had almost nothing in them. After the service I spoke to the Roman Catholic priest involved in the mass. We agreed that violence was not the solution. Emboldened by our common ground, I said that I felt the place to start was schools, that children should not be educated separately along religious lines. At which point he said that must never be allowed to happen. I spent a day following the men with plastic bags whose job it was to clear away the body parts after a bomb exploded. With mounting horror, I watched them picking hands and feet from flowering trees and bushes. I thought of a line half-remembered from Dante of a character 'torn from the scabbard of his limbs'. I came to process the muffled thuds of a bomb going off as the sound of giant doors slamming on a future without violence.

Over the years, I lost hope of ever truly understanding the conflict.

One of the key differences between ITN and the BBC was that the BBC came from a lineage of covering the news, which basically meant *telling* you about it, whereas ITN wanted to *show* you the news. They wanted to go there, talk to people, let you hear their voices, see them and come to an understanding of the situation that way. It felt messier but somehow closer to the truth. Every conversation was about how we could make a story accessible. Not just intellectually. Not just for those people that knew they were interested in current affairs. But for the person who might think they weren't. How could you find that human point of connection? How do you communicate to that person living in Norfolk that this conflict isn't some distant alien thing, that these are people like you and your family and your friends?

Always the refrain: 'But can you do it in one-minute thirty?' At Bush House there would be hour-long conversations about the fine detail of one issue. But at ITN everything was about how you were then going to communicate it. It felt bracing, and I was determined to do everything in my power to get up to speed. I spent every moment reading around a subject I was going to cover. Just before I left for Belfast I'd been sat with a friend at the Oval, explaining that I was due to be sent out to Northern Ireland. He was irate on my behalf. 'Typical,' he said. 'They get their first ever Black reporter and immediately send him out to Northern Ireland to get blown up.' I had to hurriedly explain that it was no marker of disrespect, that, in fact, I was delighted to be sent there. It meant I was at the centre of one of the biggest stories there was. I had always dreamed about being at the centre of the news. But, when I got there, I was scared by the violent reality of it. The open hatred shocked me.

I'd never heard a bomb go off. I'd never seen submachine guns. I'd never seen the politics of terror. I saw my first dead bodies. But I learned such a huge amount. It prepared me for covering all sorts of stories later. I saw for the first time that *frisson* of excitement among those who might be called upon to report terrible things. I would see it many more times – and always hated it; that queasy sense that terrible events are professionally useful. It was my first experience of war and I learned to hate it. I hated the damage it did. The destruction of everything it touched.

But the fact remained I was a Black reporter in Andersonstown and other estates in Belfast. It got me noticed. And so that was the beginning of my career on television. I was aware it was no small thing. It actually quickly became a news story that I had the job. I remember a colleague telling me there was a journalist waiting to interview me, and not really understanding why until a colleague spelled it out: 'Because you're going to be the only Black reporter on television, Trevor.' There was not a long list, even then. Barbara Blake Hannah had been, as far as I was aware, the first regular Black reporter when she'd appeared on Thames Television. But her contract had only lasted nine months after there had been complaints. If there were complaints when my reports started going out, they were kept from me. I am grateful that no one at ITN paid any attention to them.

I was aware that racism existed. But the curious thing is that television cameras create a kind of force field. You turn up with a camera and people don't really care about who you are. But they want to be on television. So perhaps if anyone was harbouring any hostility towards me, they kept it hidden so as to facilitate appearing on the television. I would sometimes have to knock on someone's door in an estate and ask to use their phone to call something in to London. The residents in these areas were not used to a Black man coming to their doors. But they were always judiciously polite.

Of course, I couldn't fail to understand at some level what it meant to others to see me on television. It was not so long since the story of the Windrush generation had begun to unfurl, many of whom had come to Britain after fighting during the Second World War, or in response to the plea for labour after the war. They were driving the buses, or working in hospitals or delivering mail. But answering this call for help did not result in fulsome gratitude, it would be fair to say. There were questions in Parliament in 1948 concerning the 'wisdom' of allowing the *Empire Windrush* to travel at all. These people arrived to the shock of the cold and the rain and a population for whom they may as well have fallen from the sky above. There was suspicion and outright hostility that played out in every area of their lives. Though many of these Caribbeans worked two or even three jobs, they were called lazy. A few years ago, I spoke to a nurse who had come over to Wales from St Lucia in 1962. She had patients tell her, 'Don't you dare put your black hand on me.' People wouldn't sit by her on the bus. But I never encountered this sort of outright hostility. I knew that, for many people, a man who looked like me and sounded like me, filling a role on television, meant something. I wasn't seen as a Trinidadian journalist; I was seen as British. Partly it was down to my accent, formed by my mother's insistence upon what is known as received pronunciation: a dialect first identified in the nineteenth century as not being connected to a locality but instead to a sort of economic context and to the metropolis. It was closely tied to the public schools of England. And so it was that English accent that made its way out to the colonies as high-status English. When mothers encouraged their children to speak 'properly' it was because that was the kind of English that represented power. My voice is that of a boy doing his best to speak in a way that won't make his mother raise her eyebrow in disapproval. But it had those echoes of Trinidad in it. Much as I had tried, I could not remove all traces. When I had been on the radio, Trinidadians had thought I was simply English. But there were traces of island in my vowels, in the rhythm and pitch and intonation. I believe my accent announced I was from a place, and perhaps Britain was ready at that point to have that voice tell it stories about itself.

Of course, at the time, I was so focused on making a success of my career that I never really thought about it. Perhaps it was that island mentality. I was determined to excel, and doing so meant being good enough at what I did to leave my island behind. To foreground my Blackness seemed at the time almost the opposite of that. It was pulling me back to the island. Pulling me back from that excellence I had aspired to, symbolised by my leaving. There was a kind of pride involved, if I am honest, which I am now more conflicted about. Had I appeared on the BBC earlier, perhaps more people would have felt more confidently that they could do the job too. But my pride drove me for the rest of my career as well, and put me in the scenarios that meant I had the career I had. I worry that it was selfish to feel this way but, like my father bringing the Finlayson boys to fish with us, I decided to be aware of it but not to care. I always felt that Britain welcomed me into its arms. For someone who already felt animated by a strong desire not to disappoint others, the idea of being some sort of figurehead or lightning rod for a whole community would have been utterly paralysing.

Certainly no colleague ever got in my way or hindered me. Quite the opposite. I remember the first editor I worked with at ITN, Nigel Ryan. He once called me up one day and said, 'Look, Trevor, I've been thinking about your career.' I almost fell out of my chair – firstly, because I wasn't really accustomed to thinking of having a career at all, more just the feeling I wanted to keep my job. And secondly that some-one else was thinking about my life in that way. It just felt so wonderfully generous. 'You should be like Sandy Gall.' He was, of course, the brilliant journalist. Nigel continued, 'You should read the news in the studio and travel the world reporting.' And I came off the phone and sat there feeling as if all my boats had come in.

The media tended not to have these structures. You got a chance, you had a go; maybe you stuck around until your face didn't fit any more. I had gravitated towards international politics, almost certainly because that felt most like the world I'd imagined all those years before, listening to my little radio.

My day job and cricket came together memorably in August 1973, on the Saturday of the Lord's Test. Coming into the Test, I was most interested in seeing Garry Sobers, who had been drafted in at late notice, in what was sure to be his last appearance. He had handed the captaincy to Rohan Kanhai the season before for the home series against Australia, which the West Indies had lost 2–0. So we were very firmly positioned as the underdogs for this tour. I was not able to make it to the first Test at the Oval, but plenty of people I knew were there in a vociferous crowd full of West Indian support to see Clive Lloyd score a glorious 132.

I was always fascinated by Lloyd. I would get to know him later, and was even lucky enough to write an official biography of him. He always found it amusing that people thought we looked alike. We were once sitting in a discotheque in Bombay when a lady asked him to dance. He said, alas, he couldn't, but pointing towards me said she should dance with 'my brother'. Another time, I was stopped in the street in Wandsworth by a woman who said, 'Mr Lloyd, I thought you were in the West Indies. It's so nice to meet you.' I never saw the likeness, personally, though I was very flattered. He was tall – 6 foot 4 – and had thick glasses to correct the short sight he received breaking up a fight when he was a boy. There was a kind of shuffling quality to him. You could forgive the bowler new to him for thinking they were up against a librarian or academic. But, by God, he could play. There was astonishing power in his bat and he knocked the ball all about the pitch. On the field, his shuffling became a lope that ate up the ground, and his huge paw-like hands never seemed to drop a catch and dispatched the ball back with lighting speed and unerring accuracy. Lloyd had grown up fast in Georgetown, British Guiana. He would later talk of how his brother and four sisters would complain when he enrolled them in fetching the balls he thwacked into neighbouring streets. You could see that boy in him when he made centuries against England in Port of Spain and in Brisbane on his Australian debut.

He had played his league cricket with Haslingden in the Lancashire League, and then for Lancashire county. He was known by his middle name, Hubert, and his role models were Worrell, Walcott, Sobers and Hall.

He was once asked what his secret was, and replied, 'If I can see the ball, I can hit it.' And boy, did he hit it – at the Oval Lloyd's 132, aided by an 80 from Alvin Kallicharran and a 72 from Keith Boyce at number nine, took the West Indies to 415. England looked to be on pace when they got to 247 for 5 but then spectacularly collapsed as Sobers and Boyce took the remaining wickets for only ten runs. It was really only Geoffrey Boycott who put up any resistance with 97. The second innings were far more even, but the damage was done. Boyce ended the match with a very impressive 11 for 147. I have always thought it must have been an impossible task to be an all-rounder after Garry Sobers.

In any other context Keith Boyce would have been a shoo-in to be a star – a fast right-arm bowler, a vicious striker of the ball and a gloriously quick and accurate fielder – but Sobers had rewritten the rules. The second Test at Edgbaston was a rather tamer affair – a draw that seemed to be taking place in treacle, but which had at its heart an admirably cussed 150 by Roy Fredericks that saw him at the crease for eight hours.

But the final Test at Lord's was all set for a glorious denouement. The players were clearly fired up by the crowd in the grandstand and out on the boundary blowing whistles, banging drums and blaring horns with every West Indian triumph – of which there were a great many over those first two days, which finished with the West Indies on 652 for 8 declared. At the centre of their batting was Kanhai with 157 and Sobers 150 not out. It was as if they were raging against the dying of the cricketing light, and they crafted their innings with utter ruthlessness. They were joined by Bernard Julien who scored a maiden century as he reached 121. This was the highest innings total ever by a West Indies side in England. England closing the Friday on 88 for 3. The Saturday began bathed in bright sun, but the West Indies bowlers continued to go after the English batters and by the middle of the afternoon session England were 206 for 8 and facing the indignity of the follow-on.

But it was then announced over the PA system that Lord's had received a telephone call warning that a bomb had been planted inside the ground. Play went on for a few minutes before the groundsman started getting the covers out. The crowd were incredulous, and the West Indian fans asked in no uncertain terms if they had lost their minds. There was not a cloud in the sky.

Eventually the crowd came streaming onto the pitch and surrounded the umpire Dickie Bird, who was perched glumly on the covers, where several fans began giving him a piece of their minds about his tendency to no-ball the West Indian bowlers. After some time Kanhai rescued him and, after about an hour as the crowd dispersed into the streets, the all-clear was finally given. It was later found to be a hoax, which led some wags to suggest it had been called in by one of the England team. It was agreed that extra time would be added on both subsequent days but instead England did follow on and lost 3 wickets, each one provoking a pitch invasion. The final wicket, when Boycott was dismissed, saw him jostled by fans.

In those days it seemed as if everyone was watching or listening to the cricket, and I was reminded of my friend who ran an office in London who said that he had been baffled that suddenly his entire office seemed to have ear plugs in, before realising that everyone was listening to the cricket.

The West Indies had seemed like they had lost their way. But where better to produce this manner of performance than Lord's? That was where the extra light and heat came from in the crowd. It just meant more to beat England. It meant that those in the crowd could walk a little taller. When they went back to their jobs on Monday morning, perhaps things wouldn't be perfect, perhaps the foreman would talk down to you, or there'd be some other reminder of your place. But the West Indies had won. You couldn't take that away.

Perhaps my abiding memory of that Test is the 150 not out by Garry Sobers. Years later it was revealed that his break at 122 for 'a stomach upset' was, in fact, the result of a hangover from the night before, in an example of whatever the opposite of nominative determinism is. Garry Sobers, whose batting style was described by Neville Cardus as having 'as little obvious propulsion as a movement of music by Mozart' ... I saw and heard him bend so many matches to his will. When you went to see a match he was playing it gave you that tingle of anticipation. You might see a moment that would echo through history. And in that Lord's innings he proved that, on a hangover, he was still better than anyone else. It was, after all, the reason that Frank Worrell made him captain. Because he already knew everything.

Years later, in 2007, when the Irish cricket team reached the final stage of the World Cup, First Minister Ian Paisley and Deputy Minister Martin McGuinness signed a joint letter congratulating the team. Yet again, I was reminded of that summer when cricket and Northern Ireland seemed inextricably aligned.

6

Grovel

'I like to think that people are building these West Indians up,' said the England captain, Tony Greig, his accent from an upbringing in South Africa never sounding more obvious. 'Because I'm not really sure they're as good as everyone thinks they are.' Then, almost as an afterthought, 'Sure, they've got a couple of fast bowlers, but . . . you must remember that if the West Indians get on top they are magnificent cricketers, but if they're down, they grovel. And I intend, with the help of Closey and a few others, to make them grovel.'

I winced when I heard it. Not because I thought it was necessarily a phrase chosen with malice. But because how could he possibly not know just how strongly that word 'grovel' would land. 'Grovel' is the essence of servitude or slavery. It is to make yourself abject. It carries within it the weight of generations of enslaved people bowing in the dust under a plantation manager or his boys. For a white man, one with a South African accent, to wield it carried within it the distant echo of the whip. If Clive Lloyd had been unsure how to motivate before, he certainly wasn't afterwards. Viv Richards would remember Lloyd telling them, 'We don't need to say much. Our man on the television just said it all for us. We know what we've gotta do.' As I would later characterise it in my biography of Richards: 'For the South African captain of an English team to publicly threaten to make the West Indies grovel was probably the closest any cricketer ever came to making a formal declaration of war.'[11] Greig's remarks were met with horror and anger, both from his teammates and the British Caribbean community, and he attempted to defuse things by apologising on the radio. But with England set to swelter under the hottest summer in more than three hundred years, and the West Indies visiting for almost the entire season, things felt primed for an intense battle.

The previous couple of years had felt difficult to spin a simple narrative from. The glory of the win at Lord's, diluted by a drawn series with England the following year, and then 1975's trip to Australia a dispiriting experience. There, an Australian attack led by Dennis Lillee and Jeff Thomson had developed an arsenal of deliveries the like of which I had certainly never seen. It had been a bruising series of matches in every sense: in those days before protective gear was common, a bouncer to the body or head was a genuinely dangerous event. And even if the ball didn't make contact, the fear it might was clearly a massively psychological distraction. The sight of an all-white Australian crowd chanting, 'Lillee, Lillee, kill, kill, kill,' as the West Indians batsmen suffered bouncer after bouncer had something deeply disquieting about it. The White Australia policy had only been officially dismantled a couple of years earlier, and there were reports that players had been called 'Black bastards' and encouraged to 'go back to the tree you came from'. In this most hostile of environments, we had lost five of the six games in the series. Words like 'pathetic' and 'capitulation' were the order of the day.

But our brilliant, shuffling, bespectacled captain, Clive Lloyd, clearly decided to fight fire with fire. He began to tour the islands looking for club players who had the raw pace to be moulded into international class bowlers. One of those was twenty-two-year-old Jamaican Michael Holding, who had made his debut in the previous tour against Australia. He'd grown up in Half Way Tree, Kingston, and would tell a story later in life of how his mother's family had disowned her because her husband's skin was too dark. He had been a 400-metre runner growing up, and his nickname was 'Whispering Death' because of how smooth and flowing his running action was. He would duck his head, then set off, easy at first before accelerating into the release. His head held high, turning slightly from side to side as if he was part thoroughbred, part cobra, the ball would leave his hand at incredible pace. The difference between the grace of the run-up and the pace of the ball was deceptive. After a batsman had faced a couple of balls, you could see the unease. The normal rules pertaining to how long you had to hit the ball didn't seem to hold firm. Shots so often seemed partially formed in response. Off the pitch, Holding was a quiet, polite man. On it, he had an iron will to win.

Then there was the Antiguan Andy Roberts. He would go on to develop a reputation as one of the fiercest fast bowlers ever produced. Roberts was a willing proponent of a slower bouncer, which he would use to lull the batter into complacency – before pitching a much faster bouncer in the same spot. This time the batsman would be out or struck. It sometimes seemed as if batsmen were acceptable collateral damage in the face of his inexorable bowling. Richard Lewis, Roberts's teammate at Hampshire, used to tell the joke that his main role as a fielder was to stand at short-leg and help disorientated batsmen back to their feet. Roberts would go on to hold a senior position in the university of pace that would characterise West Indian bowling for the next decade.

The Barbadian Wayne Daniel completed the trio: a tall, muscular bowler, for whom the price of regular no-balls was one worth paying when he got his line absolutely right. There were times watching him bowl when it seemed as if the bails might have to be collected from the neighbouring county.

There had been a small glimpse of what this team might be capable of the year before when the West Indies won the in- augural One-Day International World Cup at Lord's. Having already beaten them in the group stage, we faced Australia in the final. This time, Clive Lloyd led with a truly great cap- tain's performance, making a century off 82 balls. He seemed to pick off the formerly terrifying Australian attack with an almost relaxed swing of his bat. Arlidge said it was so fine a century he was sure he saw a policeman applauding.

Then, when Australia had belligerently begun to build momentum, Lloyd had taken over bowling duties and he and Viv Richards were responsible for the three run-outs that took the wind out of their sails. The crowd ran onto the pitch at the moment of victory. When order was restored, the MCC secretary asked Prince Philip – MCC president that year – if he would like to make a speech before giving man of the match Lloyd the cup. He reportedly replied, 'This is not an occasion for words.' I remember walking to the shops in Guildford and someone asking if I was West Indian, to which I replied yes. He then regaled me for several minutes on what a player Clive Lloyd was. My neighbours, until that point a somewhat unknown quantity, had also stopped me to talk about what a brilliant player he was. Perhaps it was a shared cause against a common enemy but it felt as if the whole of Surrey had watched the final and delighted in our victory.

It was left to the Australian media to make excuses – their team was out of season and out of practice, dropping catches they would normally take, timing their runs between the wickets poorly. But when it came down to it, we knew we had kept cooler heads.

There had been further intimations of this new attack with the Indian tour of the West Indies in early 1976. Reasoning that spin was best suited to the pitches, the first Test began with the Indians hitting the West Indian spinners all about the place. Lloyd returned to the dressing room and said, 'Gentlemen, I gave you four hundred runs to bowl at and you failed to bowl out the opposition. How many runs must I give you in the future to make sure that you get the wickets?' There was no reply. Lloyd turned his back on spin from then on – and for the final Test turned to his pace bowlers, who delivered as aggressive a display of bowling as there has ever been. One Indian batsman, Gundappa Viswanath, had his finger broken, another, Brijesh Patel, was hit in the face, and then Anshuman Gaekwad was hit behind the left ear and had to be taken to hospital. The Indian captain declared their innings over and asked that five Indian batsmen should be recorded as 'absent hurt'. *Wisden* famously described the Indian team as resembling Napoleon's troops retreating from Moscow as they waited to catch the plane home. Official complaints went in, with Gavaskar accusing the West Indies of 'barbarism'. Lloyd shrugged it off as all part of the game. The difference in outlook when it was the West Indies bowling rather than on the receiving end did not go unnoticed by many of my West Indian cricketing friends.

So, come the tour of England, the strategy of riling up the West Indian bowlers felt especially curious. And if we had talent with the ball, at bat we certainly had grounds for optimism. We had Clive Lloyd, of course, who seemed to be gaining authority every time he went to the crease. But there were two more reasons I felt especially optimistic.

One was named Viv Richards. The Antiguan was born into a cricketing dynasty. His father was the Antiguan fast bowler Malcolm Richards; his brothers played cricket for Antigua. He was a gifted athlete and had grown up playing football and cricket and was rumoured to have been good enough at both to play internationally – however, thankfully, he chose cricket. He was one of those cricketers who sometimes arrive fully formed, announcing himself on his debut tour of India with a 192 of sweet brutality. I remember him walking out at M. Chinnaswamy Stadium as if he were wandering out to the shops for a paper. In time, I would come to think there were few sights finer in the whole of cricket than Viv Richards strolling out chewing gum. He walked to the wicket like a god. He projected the air that bowling towards him was an impertinence, the sheer swagger of his self-possession perceptible even through the television screen. Then, feet planted wide apart, that almost theatrical exaggerated backlift ... It didn't seem to matter which form of bowling was employed, Richards had a shot ready, which would be played with an attitude tinged with almost disdain. Anything short was hooked with routine excellence. If the bowler went full and straight he'd flick it away leg-side like a man at a bar swatting a mosquito. One of his favoured shots was to drive anything pitched outside off-stump through mid-wicket. He would just attack relentlessly, whoever it was, whatever the state of the pitch or the ball, or the game. He went after every ball like it had insulted his mother. He was one of those batsmen who threatened to clear not just the boundary but the ground. By the end of his career he had pioneered a style of batting, hitting across the line in a way that broke many of the old rules. But it was Richards's presence that made him special. I once saw him in the flesh, hit by a vicious bouncer on the side of the head. He hardly seemed to acknowledge it, but the next ball he hooked for an enormous six. Then he just stood there calmly, looking at the bowler. With some batsmen there is a sense that their innings are for themselves, their own glory, their own numbers, their own place in the pantheon. But somehow with Viv Richards it never felt like that. He knew that the best way of buying his bowlers enough time to get the other team out was to make a big score quickly. Perhaps his statistics would have been even better if that wasn't the case.

The second reason for optimism lay in another debutant from the Indian tour, Gordon Greenidge, who'd scored 93 and then 107 on his debut in the 1974 tour. He had been born in Barbados and raised by his grandmother from the age of eight until fourteen when his mother sent for him in England. At school he faced racist bullying, was excluded from the cricket team and left with no qualifications. But he joined Hampshire to play county cricket when he was seventeen, as well as painting the ground's seating. His choosing to play for the West Indies always felt like it had a special charge. He was a sublime batsman in the true romantic sense of the word, in that his shots were beautiful but not a little terrifying. It was a common refrain at the height of his powers to describe his shots like a lion or a tiger completing its kill. I think he hit the ball harder than any man I've seen before or since. There were times when, had the ball disappeared in a puff of red smoke, one would not have been too surprised. He could pull and hook with equal parts precision and force. There was a special kind of geometry to his strokes. They jointed the field like a butcher's knife.

Greenidge had been one of the batters who had suffered most in the cauldron of racist invective and pace bowling in Melbourne a year earlier. The World Cup had been a quiet one for him but, back in England a year on, with Greig's words ringing in his ears, it felt all set up for a response by him.

The first Test was at Trent Bridge, and even though Viv Richards made a magnificent 232 he was eventually caught out by Tony Greig, which received an enormous jeer. The standing ovation from the West Indies fans was like a wave of sound, and was perhaps even more firmly delivered because of who had made the catch. It was an odd match, as England patiently batted their way to a draw. It was by no means a disaster, but there were those who felt that perhaps we had let the occasion get to us a little.

The second Test at Lord's saw Viv Richards sit out the match through injury. A subdued West Indies and a washout on the third day's play resulted in another draw. There was then to be a gap of three weeks before the next Test at Old Trafford.

June and into July saw a heatwave that felt like the English weather was determined to put out the welcome mat for the West Indies. Indeed, temperatures in Port of Spain and Manchester were within a single degree of each other. And how often can one say that? As I sat, with the windows open in an attempt to coax the still Guildford air to move through my house, I could hear the cricket on the televisions in houses all around me. I remember having polite conversations with neighbours at the time who felt that the West Indies had perhaps been overhyped. I had politely reminded them that this was the first match that we would be at full strength. Clive Lloyd won the toss and chose to bat first.

Things did not get off to a particularly auspicious start. Roy Fredericks, Viv Richards, Alvin Kallicharran and Clive Lloyd were dismissed and we found ourselves 26 for 4. At this point, I rather regretted my fighting talk earlier in the week. Thankfully, Gordon Greenidge had come to play. Over the next 198 balls he hit eighteen fours and reached a total of 134. I couldn't take my eyes off him. Here was batting with a kind of ice-cold fury. Later, he would say of his attitude to batting, 'I felt that to forcefully go at what I was doing, to attack, was a way of letting out that anger. It wouldn't be right to take it out on a fellow human being, though you felt like that at times, but I'm sure gonna take it out on five-and-a-half ounces.'[12] It was as if every boarding-school taunt was being repaid with interest, with the ball as his interlocutor. He was supported by Collis King, who made 32 as the West Indies eventually reached a total of 211.

Then it was time for England to face the West Indian bowlers. Brian Close and David Steel were out at 37 for 2 but, as the day finished, things still felt finely poised. It would not be beyond this talented England team to dig out a draw again. I slept in the warm Guildford night and dreamed of my childhood.

The next day was glorious. The sky a bright, light blue. It is rare that I have felt true pity for a West Indian opponent, but I did that day. Holding was imperious, taking 5 wickets for 17. Roberts took 3 for 22 and Daniel took 2 for 13. David Steele was the only batsmen to trouble double figures as England were all out for 71. It was as close to utter domination as you will ever see. With every joyous leap of a successful claim it felt as if something was being exorcised. A tightness, a heaviness fell away from the team. As the West Indians in the crowd jumped and waved and cried out in joy, the sheer unending progress of run-up, bowl, claim, shout, became hypnotic. When Tony Greig was bowled for a grand total of 9, the West Indians could be heard to shout out the word 'grovel' in utter primal delight. Too often before that point, the phrase 'calypso cricket' had been used as a somewhat patronising stereotype, insinuating a lack of discipline, focus or mentality; of only playing the game for fun. But anyone who knew their calypsos properly knew they had bite. The calypso was politics, where politics found expression in the region, where you could say things you could not say else-where. Here was true calypso cricket, biting as satire, with a political intensity. Every member of the team seemed to be driven by a desire to show they were the equal, man for man, of their opponents. Not only that, they were writing a history; not the history of Drake or Nelson that we had all been taught, but their own history. They were determined to play in a manner that would inscribe this game so deeply it would never be forgotten. England would be dismissed in 32 and a half overs for a total of 71 runs.

This time around there would be no early collapse. Over the remainder of the second and most of third day, what the West Indies had started with the ball, they continued with the bat. Fredericks scored 50, Greenidge 101, Viv Richards 135 and Clive Lloyd 43. When I recall that innings now, it is the flash of their bats in the bright sun, and the control of it – the discipline; a perfect meeting of creativity and ruthlessness – that lingers. When we declared on 411 for 5 near the end of the third day, it left England chasing a target of 552 to win. They would need to survive two days to draw. They managed to survive for 63 and a half overs and the rain even briefly came to their aid on the fourth day. But on the final day, all it took was 20 balls for England to be out for 126.

We had won the third Test by 425 runs. I was full of nervous energy after the match, pacing about. I had been moved by what I saw in ways that, at the time, I didn't fully understand. It was partly the noise from the West Indians in the crowd. There was an intensity that spoke to what this meant to the entire West Indian community. To have beaten England on their own turf, like this!

The fourth Test at Headingley was *only* won by 55 runs,

with some brilliant batting by Greenidge and Fredericks. It would have been in normal circumstances an utterly thrilling match and indeed the roar when it became clear that Greig's words had been shoved down his throat was enormous. But after the enormity of Old Trafford it couldn't help but feel just a little quotidian in comparison.

It meant, though, that we would win the series whatever happened at the Oval in the final Test. But it was expected that England, a wounded beast, would fight furiously for their pride. The atmosphere at the Oval was astonishing. It was more like a home match for the West Indies team. It felt as if the whole of the West Indian community in Brixton had turned up with drums and whistles. The noise was astonishing. The outfield was brown, the wicket dry and powdered. It was thought to be a pitch that would very much favour the batsmen. The West Indies won the toss and batted first. Losing Gordon Greenidge for LBW a couple of overs in felt potentially damaging. But then Viv Richards stepped up. And he stayed there the entire day. He made 200 runs that first day – there are no words to describe it. He didn't seem human, he seemed geological. A mountain in a rainstorm. Nothing the English bowlers tried had any effect. I have been in crowds when something truly special happens in sport. There is a kind of mania at the sheer brilliance of what you're seeing. You could hear laughter at points when he thwacked a particularly impudent ball over the boundary. I don't think I've ever seen a field run so much and achieve so little.

The next day, he went back up and made another 91. Over almost eight hours at the crease he reached a total of 291 from 386 balls, including thirty-eight fours. If there has ever been finer individual batting performance in Test cricket, I don't know of it. Aided by 71 for Roy Fredericks, a 70 from Lawrence Rowe and an 84 from our captain, West Indies finished the first innings when they declared on an astonishing 687.

England's first innings was defined by a brilliant 203 from Dennis Amiss. The wicket was so dry and dusty it felt like beach cricket at points. And Clive Lloyd's decision to go with only pace in these conditions looked as if it might have backfired, as the pitch was just too predictable and anything even slightly short was swatted away with ease. However, Holding came to the wicket and the pace seemed to leap up. He would take 8 wickets, all either bowled or leg-before. When he bowled Greig after a succession of balls that might have come under the category of GBH, there was a pitch invasion. Dickie Bird would later say it was the most fantastic spell of fast bowling he had ever seen. Knowing that Holding was exhausted, there was to be no follow-on and Roy Fredericks and Gordon Greenidge added another 182 between them in just 32 overs. At one point Tony Greig went towards one of the sections of the crowd packed with the most West Indies fans and went down on his hands and knees in front of them. When the innings was closed it felt more in a spirit of mercy than sporting strategy. Amiss and Bob Woolmer got 43 on the board before the end of the fourth day. With the pitch as it was, I couldn't escape the sense that, after all that extraordinary play, the most likely outcome was a draw. This would by no means be a terrible outcome, but offended my childhood sense of fairness. To have a batsman nearly score a triple century, to have a single bowler take 8 wickets and yet for them to only draw, it just didn't feel quite right.

The next morning Holding was as near perfect as you could ever want. He was poetry, he was song. There was no threatening the batsmen; he simply bowled fast, full and with perfect line. Alan Knott put up resistance but the innings finished with Holding taking 6 for 57, to put alongside his 8 for 92 in the first innings. We had won the match by 231 runs, and the Test series 3–0. Not since Donald Bradman in 1948 had England faced this score in a home series.

The West Indies would also go on to win the one-day series 3–0. It was a series where everywhere one looked there were performances of brilliance, where the remarkable was made to seem routine. And it had at the heart of it an iron core of discipline and determination. With every sinew and every fibre of their being they showed that there could be no worse description than 'grovel'. Perhaps it had been deployed to try to make our players lose control. Instead they stood tall, they strutted, they strolled; they were poetry in motion.

Thirty-five years later Michael Holding would be interviewed during a break in play for rain, when he began to talk about race. He remembered his schooldays, never being taught about achievements by Black people. He described history written by the conqueror. By those who harmed, not those who received harm. And I thought about how what that team accomplished was to create cricketing heroes the equivalent of Drake, Nelson or Shakespeare. He spoke of being followed around in shops because you are Black. How different life was. He broke down in tears thinking of it. I watched it and I thought about what he carried inside him on that day when he bowled as close to perfection as I had ever seen.

I was just beginning the period of my life when I would travel the world on the trail of some of the biggest global news stories. But, during that longest and hottest of summers, something I will never forget occurred.

7

Just Not Cricket

November 1978

'How about this, hey, Trevor?' Johnny Woodcock couldn't help but laugh. It was November 1978 and we were walking through a crowd more like a carnival than on their way to a cricket game in Sydney. I stopped a woman whose face was painted with the Australian flag and asked if she was a cricket fan. She laughed and said, 'Not normally, but I am now.' Johnny harrumphed at this. I was genuinely fascinated, but very much in a minority.

The previous year, the Sex Pistols had released 'God Save the Queen', but for those of us who worshipped at the church of willow on leather, something equally iconoclastic happened that year too. In May, the Australian Kerry Packer held a press conference where he announced the signing of thirty-five of the world's best cricketers to play in a series of internationals in Australia that winter.

Packer had not originally wanted to shake cricket's foundations; he'd wanted to buy them. He'd made an offer of $1.5 million Australian dollars for the rights to televise

Australia's home Test matches. But, as always, they had been sold to ABC in what he felt was an under-the-table way. Packer's solution to being kept out of that game was to create his own. He signed on Tony Greig to recruit more players and lead the team, and Greig was promptly dropped as captain by the England Cricket Council. John Arlott called it 'a circus'. Packer's series was immediately seen as a mortal threat to Test cricket. The initial list of signatories included people like John Snow, Alan Knott and Derek Underwood from England and, of special note to me, Viv Richards and Andy Roberts from the West Indies – but it would go on to include, among many others, Clive Lloyd, Wayne Daniel, Roy Fredericks, Gordon Greenidge, Michael Holding and Rohan Kanhai. On offer were salaries thirty times what cricketers were earning elsewhere.

Perhaps it was my upbringing playing the most non-regulation cricket with tree branches, perhaps it was my memories of pretending my father was out for dinner as he broke the picket line, but something inside me bristled a little when I heard the argument that cricket's immortal soul was being sullied by crude commerce. You cannot, of course, escape cricket's roots in the class of man who did not need to sully themselves with such things. You don't play a game that lasts five days if you have to be at the factory for a shift tomorrow morning. Cricket thrived in colonial soil because much of the actual labour was carried out a long way away from you, overseen by others, leaving you plenty of time for sport. It is no coincidence, then, that it was West Indian men who were targeted by Packer. Yes, they were box office, but they were men receptive to a payday. The ineffable coarsening of cricket's soul was certainly worth thinking about. Being able to provide for one's family was a far more compelling argument.

Kerry Packer, a hugely successful media tycoon, wasn't very well known in Britain before that original press conference, though I had heard many stories about him by that time. He loved gambling and was famous for betting millions of dollars on single roulette spins or hands of cards. He was said to have lost £19 million in one night of poker at the Ritz. When he won, he was famously generous, paying off the mortgages of cocktail waitresses and donating chips to croupiers. He had once offered to bet $100 million on the flip of a coin. One night, he turned up with some friends looking for dinner at a pub in the village he was staying in, only to be told they were too late and turfed out. So on to the next pub, where the kitchen was also closed but the owner offered to make them some ham sandwiches to go with their drinks. When the bill for £100 arrived, Packer wrote them a cheque for £100,000. His only request was before they cashed it they show it to the landlord of the other pub who had turfed them out. But he was a hugely successful and ruthless businessman.

Packer felt certain about two things. One, the people who marketed cricket were not doing the best possible job. And two, the players were underpaid. This was his opportunity. At first, the plan was for six Tests and six one-day matches between an Australian XI and a Rest of the World XI. West Indian cricketers were used to travelling to another country to play their cricket. But the English and Australian authorities reacted aggressively, seeing it as an act of war. The West Indies Cricket Board were unable to convince Packer of a more placatory approach and instead they agreed to try to 'kill off' Packer.

By the time the first fixture was played on 2 December 1977, Packer's breakaway tournament had been named World Series Cricket and there were seventy or so players now involved for six 'Supertests' involving Indian, West Indian, Australian and Rest of the World XIs, as well as thirteen one-day matches. At first, the response from the public was underwhelming, with small crowds and traditionalists comforting themselves that this wasn't what fans wanted. The Australian cricket authorities had refused to make traditional venues available and banned their players from selection for their teams while they appeared in these fixtures. Instead, Packer had to repurpose Perth's Gloucester Park racing ground. In Melbourne it was the VFL Park. People might not have come to the first couple of matches, but the sheer concentration of top-class cricketers produced its own gravity. Packer had gone after the biggest hitters and the fastest bowlers for a reason. It was an Andy Roberts bouncer that really changed things. It hit the Australian David Hookes in the jaw and was captured in graphic detail by Packer's film cameras. If prior to this there had been something of the exhibition about the series, this seemed to say that the stakes were very real. The wickets were made or grown and carefully transferred into the venues, and it was generally agreed they were extremely good.

These matches produced very good television adverts and rethought what the role of cricket commentary was. It was utterly different from the way that cricket had been treated previously. Everything was about speed, strength and adrenaline. Packer was hugely demanding. He made it clear that if you weren't prepared to give your absolute all for the matches, you'd be on a Qantas flight home the next day. The matches were physically and psychologically intense.

Though the first series hadn't been an unqualified success, interest was growing. In March the following year the official Australian team, still refusing to pick anyone with a World Series Cricket contract, travelled to the West Indies. The West Indies Cricket Board made a decision to pick their WSC-contracted players, but then deselected them for the third Test. This would eventually lead Clive Lloyd to resign and every WSC cricketer to state that they were not available for selection. Gradually, there was seen to be a thawing towards Packer and WSC, as all around the world the top players were rumoured to be signing options. Packer created a second tier of competition, which included recently retired big-name players. He was also able to convince the authorities to allow them to play WSC games at the Sydney Cricket Ground.

That carnival crowd we were walking through in Sydney was the almost forty-five thousand who would turn out to the watch the first day–night match in a traditional cricket ground. I remember very little about the actual cricket other than Viv Richards being bowled by Dennis Lillee and Gordon Greenidge being the best of the West Indian batsmen. But the crowd were hugely engaged. The match lasted for a little over five and a half hours, and the Australians won. Though I didn't quite view it as the sacrilege some did, I couldn't help but miss some elements of Test cricket, namely the variety of play, that sense of a tactical battle. This was all boom and bang. But it was cricket. There was a familiar essential joy about it. Perhaps it reminded me of my childhood games. Perhaps it was looking around at a very different sort of crowd and seeing them realise what the fuss was about. There were women and children. You could go to the cricket after work. The ball was a different colour, the kits were a different colour. You couldn't look around that crowd and not think that Packer was clearly onto something.

Only a few days later, an under-strength official Australian side was thrashed by the English, watched by tiny crowds. The Supertest final had almost twice as many spectators. The writing was on the wall. There was then a World Series Cricket tour of the West Indies by a WSC Australian team. The standard was incredibly high, with participants saying it was the highest they had ever faced. A truce was hastily brokered. Packer got his broadcast rights.

In 1979 the world saw a team that was essentially the West Indian WSC team arrive in England for the second Cricket World Cup. The West Indies beat India in their first match at Edgbaston by 9 wickets, with our fast bowlers taking the first 5 wickets for fewer than 80 runs. They managed to rally and finish on 190, but Greenidge hit a hundred and the West Indies won for the loss of only one wicket. A week later at Trent Bridge, a 73 not out by Clive Lloyd and a 65 by Greenidge was enough for our bowlers to get New Zealand out with 32 runs to spare.

The semi-final at the Oval saw a total of 293 look to be too much for Pakistan, and the West Indies won by 43.

The final, between the West Indies and England at Lord's, had echoes of the Oval in 1976. England won the toss and elected to put the West Indies into bat. This looked like a masterstroke from Mike Brearley when Greenidge, Haynes, Kallicharan and Lloyd were out for 99 after an hour and a half. Even Viv Richards didn't quite seem to have got his eye in. Then Collis King came out to bat. He was a solid all-rounder who'd made his debut in 1976 against England, but he was certainly not a player anyone was pinning their hopes upon. Richards reportedly told him to take it easy as they had plenty of time. But King was in no mood to wait. His first ball was from Ian Botham, which he cut for four. Due to an injury to Bob Willis, England were only playing four bowlers, with Geoffrey Boycott, Wayne Larkins and Peter Willey to make up the extra 12 overs. Richards would later talk about the 'silly little smirk' on Boycott's face as he bowled to King. But that smirk was to disappear as the ball flew all around the ground. Richards described his role as to work around him 'while the fire raged'. King got 19 before lunch. Then came out after lunch and really got going. He scored a further 65, including three sixes. It had taken them seventy-seven minutes to add 139 to the score. Richards then took up the cause and would end on 138 not out. But he was left in no doubt who had turned the day. 'I scored 138,' he said, 'but it was Collis who came in and took charge.' England were not able to score at the required rate, and once Brearley and Boycott were dismissed they lost their last 8 wickets for 12 runs in 25 balls. England were all out for 194 and the West Indies won by 92 runs.

This was, in so many ways, a victory forged in Australia. The Packer revolution had only lasted two seasons, but it changed cricket for ever.

I had my own brush with the limelight that year too. By this point, as well as reporting from around the world, I had also begun to read the news. And then the wonderful young comedian Lenny Henry debuted an affectionate portrayal of me that he would come to call Trevor McDoughnut. The following year I appeared on *Tiswas* to meet the other Trevor. For the first time, I would have people greet me in the street. At first I found it utterly strange. But after the first couple of times passed, and they didn't say I was the worst broadcaster they had ever had the misfortune to experience, I decided it wasn't the most onerous thing to put up with. I remember once walking down the street with my son, who must have been four or five then, and somebody on a bicycle came off the main road, went onto the pavement and slapped me on the back and said, 'Hello, Trev.' My son said, 'How does that man know us?'.

It was in 1979 that the English journalist Scyld Berry first coined the nickname 'The Four Horsemen of the Apocalypse' for the West Indies pace bowlers. For that competition Andy Roberts and Michael Holding were joined by the 6-foot-8 Barbadian Joel Garner, whose distinctive high-arm action and height served him so well in limited-overs cricket. Also Colin Croft from British Guiana, who was intimidating, and whose passion to win burned as brightly as we had ever seen. Of course, even as far back as Learie Constantine, George Francis and Herman Griffith we'd had players who were as fast as anyone around. There were players, too, like Manny Martindale, Leslie Hylton, Hines Johnson, Roy Gilchrist and, of course, the brilliant Wes Hall and Charlie Griffith. But there was something about this four that felt so considered and deliberate. It wasn't simply that they had physical gifts – it had long been grudgingly accepted that West Indian players possessed those – but it was the way those gifts were deployed. It became clear that Lloyd's strategy of unrelenting pace and brilliant aggressive batting was perfectly suited for limited-overs cricket. To a large extent he had future-proofed it.

1979 was also, in many ways, the high-water mark of Clive Lloyd's captaincy (although there would be subsequent triumphs). Lloyd's attitude towards World Series Cricket was simple: he could never understand why anyone wouldn't have joined the WSC. The economic life of a West Indian cricketer was always precarious. There was no full-time cricket. Even the very best players from the islands would finish their careers then need to work afterwards. Sometimes they bought pubs, or retrained or found work, if they were lucky, as coaches, or in the world of broadcast media. But for Lloyd, it boiled down to merely the recognition that professionals should be able to earn a living. Perhaps for those of us whose relatives were enslaved people and indentured servants, the idea of fair remuneration felt more urgent. It also felt revolutionary for those players to be involved in shaping this new version of cricket. Not to have it passed on to us by former colonial masters, but to be brought into its evolution at the same stage. Lloyd constantly advocated for more recognition and more financial support for West Indies cricketers. He would captain the West Indies to victory over Australia, all the sweeter as revenge for that brutal humiliation in 1975–76. But in the mini-series against New Zealand in 1980 there was controversy as complaints over the umpiring led to Michael

Holding kicking the stumps out of the ground at the batsmen's end and Colin Croft shouldering the umpire as he ran past. Lloyd refused to talk to the umpire. Lloyd was fiercely loyal to his players and refused to criticise them. He was loved by his players and respected. As men like Constantine and Worrell had done before him, he acted as an exemplar for the men who came after him.

Lloyd would later say, 'When you consider our painful history, the bitter impositions forced upon those who came before us and the particular ordeals that the inhabitants of the Caribbean had to overcome each day of their lives, you can begin to understand why winning cricket matches for the West Indies meant so much to us all – those at home and those making their way around the world. Excellence had arrived. Our collective and individual skills had at last been recognised and could not be denied any longer. We represented people who could make a difference.'[13]

8

Rebel Tours

A West Indian Team Tours Apartheid South Africa, 1982–83

'I'm sorry, sir, you can't come in.'

I smiled politely at the waiter who had come forwards quickly to meet me as soon as we'd entered the room. He vibrated with solicitous politeness as only a white South African enforcing apartheid in 1984 could.

I played dumb. 'But you have plenty of tables.'

His eyes flicked between the rest of us and me. 'I'm afraid we don't have an . . . international licence.' I had known this was coming. Indeed, if I was honest, I had come to this restaurant in a spirit of mischief. The euphemistic 'international licence' simply meant restaurants where Black people were allowed to eat.

By this time, I'd been lucky enough to follow Nigel Ryan's advice, and alongside my reports from around the world, I'd also begun to read the news. Before I'd left England, some of my colleagues expressed worry about my travelling to South Africa, and I joked, 'I don't know what you mean – most people there are Black.'

I was in South Africa to report on the introduction of the Tricameral Parliament. This was essentially a way for the minority white population of South Africa to nominally give power to the 'Coloured' and Indian population of South Africa. The Indians had arrived in South Africa in a similar manner to those in Trinidad, though their roots went back further, into the mid-seventeenth century. 'Coloured' was a legally defined racial classification, which essentially meant anyone who was not white but who did not speak any of the indigenous languages. Though it was being celebrated as a step in the right direction, increasing parliamentary representation, the new parliament seemed to me a clear strategy by the white minority to splinter a potential shared political identity; to recruit the Indian population with crumbs from the table. I said, 'You're being bought off.' This didn't go down too well.

But the government, perhaps from arrogance or delusion, were proud of their Tricameral and genuinely felt that if you went to South Africa and saw things for yourself, you would change your mind; you would agree that this was, in fact, the best way for them to organise their society. The idea that I would travel through the country viewing signs that said: 'White Area, Caution: Beware of Natives', or a playground announcing it was for 'European Mothers Only' – that I would see the segregation of everything, from telegraph offices to toilets – and come out nodding in approval seemed to be absurd. The vast wound of apartheid found its expression in a hundred thousand daily cuts.

F. W. de Klerk would go on to play his important part in dismantling apartheid, but back then, when I asked him why he did not give rights to the Black population, he replied that they had their 'homelands' and there they could 'look after their own affairs'. I remember being chilled by that euphemism. What he was referring to was the homelands, or Bantustans, which had been an attempt by the government to give the illusion of political equality to the Black population. They were areas where the majority of Black South Africans were forcibly moved. They were organised along tribal origin, so if someone was of Zulu descent, they were sent to KwaZulu. Ciskei and Transkei were created for the Xhosa people. These areas were geographically separate, in an attempt to splinter any possibility for a shared Black identity. They were said to be independent from South Africa, and each had an independent government. The argument was that Black people had citizenship and civil and political rights in these homelands, though they didn't in South Africa, or 'White South Africa', as it was almost always referred to.

The homelands, of course, also contained the poorest farmland. Any farmland Black communities may have owned prior to resettlement was taken from them and sold at below market rate to white farmers. This meant that the majority of the population had to go and work in the cities of White South Africa. They were set up to fail, which would then reinforce the argument that Black South Africans were not 'ready' to govern themselves.

It was remarkable to me that the government thought I would travel through the country, witnessing the blot on humanity that was apartheid and come away from it sympathetic to their cause. To stand in that restaurant, to look a man in the eye as he used euphemism to politely turn me away, I saw the centre of a machine that stripped humanity from all it touched. A couple of days earlier, some white South Africans who were hosting me for lunch paused and had a casual discussion, in the same tone they might use to discuss travel logistics, over where they might be able to take me for a meal. Which restaurant would allow a Black man into it? They were trapped in this system too. The banality of evil requires mutual and continual participation in the system. To stop is to risk admitting that you have treated humans badly. They must be dehumanised as things, problems, statistics, objects. If they are then the way you treat them is not evil – because to objectify, to treat things like things, is not evil. And if you never admit they are people (not things) then you can continue to treat them any way you want.

It was an especially charged time for me to be in South Africa, as the year before a party of seventeen West Indian cricketers had travelled there – against the advice of their own governments, cricket's world governing body and the UN – and toured South Africa.

Although, as always, I had sympathy for their need to support their families, I saw this as very different from Mr Packer's offer. Many players refused to tour South Africa. The organiser put an open cheque on the table in front of Viv Richards and said, 'Fill in whatever you want.' But he saw it as 'selling his soul' and refused at any price. In the end, the team, captained by Lawrence Rowe, was shorn of a great many of the stars and filled with understudies and those at the end of their careers. There was talk of using sport to break down barriers. But it never sat at all well with me. Though there was the irony that the large crowds that turned up witnessed non-negotiable

Black excellence, the West Indian cricketers were not the only 'Rebel Team' to tour South Africa either, with England and Australian rebel teams touring during the decade.

The issue stretched back to the 1960s. South Africa had become a republic in 1961. Though the country officially left the ICC at the same time, they continued to play cricket without much impediment. In 1968, what became known as the D'Oliveira affair blew up in regard to a proposed England tour of South Africa. Basil D'Oliveira was a 'Coloured' South African who was unable to play cricket in South Africa. He wrote to John Arlott to ask for help in finding an English club, which eventually bore fruit. He moved to England, played for Worcestershire and had represented England at cricket since 1966. The South African government let it be known that they would cancel the tour if D'Oliveira were selected. When D'Oliveira was not selected, with the justification that it was a purely sporting decision, there was massive public outcry, and the tour was cancelled.

I had made a programme in the winter of 1970 for the BBC Caribbean Service about the South African tour of England, which was receiving protests. I had interviewed the Conservative shadow attorney general, Sir Peter Rawlinson, who was very much of the mind that the protesters should face injunctions. The conversation was not so much about South African society but about hippies and their right, or lack thereof, to protest. Mike Brearley put out a statement saying that South Africa should not be allowed to tour. John Arlott said he would not broadcast on any tour match. I was in the audience the day that Home Secretary James Callaghan asked the MCC to withdraw their invitation.

In 1971–72 Don Bradman was the chairman of the Australian Cricket Board. He had always maintained that sport and politics should be kept separate. Public opinion largely reflected that what was happening in South Africa shouldn't impact Australia. There had been massive protests in 1971 when the South African rugby team had toured Australia. Bradman wrote to Meredith Burgmann, a protester who had been sent to prison, to ask why she felt so strongly about this issue. Eventually he travelled to South Africa to meet Prime Minister John Vorster. Vorster, of course, was a former member of the Ossewabrandwag, a South African group that officially supported pro-Nazi activities. Bradman's first question was reportedly, 'Why don't you choose Blacks in the team?' Vorster began to explain to Bradman that Blacks could understand something like rugby, but they couldn't handle the mental and physical intricacies of cricket. Bradman's answer was, 'Have you heard of Garry Sobers?' 'We will not play them until they choose a team on a non-racial basis,' Bradman concluded. Instead, a 'Rest of the World' team, captained by Garry Sobers, toured. Sobers scored 254 and Bradman said it was the best innings by a batsman ever seen in Australia.

Then, in 1981, what became known as the Jackman affair had threatened England's tour of the West Indies when it transpired that a late addition to the tour, the bowler Robin Jackson, had spent the British winters playing and coaching in South Africa and Rhodesia. The Guyanese government were particularly keen to adhere to the 1977 Gleneagles Agreement wherein Commonwealth leaders had vowed to 'combat the evil of apartheid by withholding any form of support for, and by taking every practical step to discourage, contact or competition by their nationals with sporting organisations, teams or sportsmen from South Africa'. So they revoked Jackman's visa. (England's squad also included Barbados-born Roland Butcher, England's first Black player.) The England Cricket Council were unwilling to field a team in this context and the second Test was cancelled and the entire tour looked like it might be too. However, the governments of Antigua, Barbados, Jamaica and Montserrat met and agreed that individuals acting alone fell outside of the Gleneagles Agreement and so did not revoke Jackman's visa.

It was against this background that Michael Holding bowled what has been called the greatest over in the history of Test cricket. At wicket was Geoffrey Boycott, one of the England players who would tour apartheid South Africa; 14 March 1981 at the Kensington Oval, Barbados, marked the second day of the third Test. The West Indies had been dismissed for 265 and Boycott, perhaps the purest expression of Yorkshire bloody mindedness there has ever been, was key to the England hopes of winning. Boycott was a man who once professed astonishment to me about French people speaking 'bloody French'. He practised in the nets with such single-minded intensity that the other players famously got sick of things so, one afternoon, Boycott procured some local schoolkids to come and bowl at him. The legend is that they lost interest before he did. He was forty by this time and had added 'the dying of the light' to things he was raging against. Boycott had an average of 51 over his three tours of the West Indies and, for a variety of reasons, his was a prized wicket.

Clive Lloyd had once dropped a catch from him and told the press it was deliberate as Boycott was batting so slowly they wanted to keep him there because he wasn't scoring very many runs. I'm not sure how true that was, or if it was just an attempt to wind up Boycott. For his part, Holding had been struggling with his action after a knee injury, but after some intense work with Andy Roberts he was feeling like he could rely on his famously elegant action again.

The first ball was pitched outside off-stump at serious pace. Boycott prodded but missed. The second was similar to the first, but came back in and hit Boycott just above the hip. There was applause from the West Indies fans that had climbed onto the tin roofs of the stand to get a better look. The third ball received a roar as a short, nasty bouncer was fended off Boycott's throat, looping up and landing short of gully. Boycott had been formed in the days before helmets and remembered batting against Fred Trueman when, 'If you took your eye off the ball and got hit without a helmet you were off to hospital so you better learn quick.'[14] The fourth ball seemed like it landed in almost exactly the same spot as the third, and was again swatted by the batsman from his throat like someone desperately swatting at a hornet. The crowd were coming to the boil by this point.

The last ball of the over. And then the safety of the non-striker's end awaited. Boycott raised his bat down, held perhaps ready to swat away another bouncer, but this ball was fuller and the quickest of all. But before Boycott had even thought to jam his bat down, the off-stump was cartwheeling 30 yards behind him. Such is the joy that only a fast ball can deliver. The crowd paused for a moment then processed what they'd seen, and there was an enormous roar. Boycott walked off with an air of almost existential puzzlement.

My reports from South Africa that year were not entirely well received by the South African authorities. One, where I pointed out that police violence not available elsewhere had managed equality between the races, received special opprobrium: 'We assumed Mr McDonald would report facts, not editorialise.' A few years later, in 1986, the erstwhile Australian prime minister, Malcolm Fraser, visited Nelson Mandela in prison. Mandela's first question was reportedly, 'Is Don Bradman alive?' When Mandela was released, Fraser presented him with a bat with an inscription from Bradman: 'To Nelson Mandela. In recognition of a great unfinished innings – Don Bradman.'

I was lucky enough to be the first person to interview Nelson Mandela when he was released. The authorities were terrified of what would happen when he physically moved through the country as he travelled from Cape Town to Soweto. They imagined anger, violence and rioting; some manifestation of revenge for the twenty-seven years of his life that had been stolen. Instead, there was an explosion of joy and hope.

With one eye on the headlines, I was keen that we might get a soundbite of him telling me about the appalling conditions he had faced: 'Mandela tells McDonald: "I was beaten every day."' But every time I tried to take the conversation in that direction, he would instead talk about the future: 'That is the past. We must talk about the future.' Over the years, I was lucky enough to meet him many more times. It is not a new thing to profess admiration for Nelson Mandela, of course. But to consistently see a man refuse anger and choose hope – to look forwards and not back; to place one foot after the other and, with each step, continue that long walk – was one of the great privileges of my life. The fact that he never should have had to undertake that long walk does not negate the nobility of his actions.

He told me that he believed that if you were prepared to sit down and talk seriously, anything was possible. I challenged him on that. I said I was sure there were things that were possible, but there were core beliefs that were too set, too fixed, as well. And he said, no, 'Everything is possible.'

When he became president in 1994, he came into his office and there were not surprisingly a lot of white assistants employed. And he deliberately went round and said to them, 'I want you all to stay because I will need the help of everybody. If this experience is going to work.' He said the secret was compromise. They took twenty-seven years of his life and he was willing to, of all things, compromise.

We anchored the *News at Ten* from Soweto, and near the end of an interview with Desmond Tutu, I said to him, 'This man might not be able to accomplish everything he needs to.' 'Man, this is no time for questions,' he replied. 'He's out, man. And it's glorious.' And he put his arms around me and did a Desmond Tutu jig. I have always been more of an observer than a dancer. But even I moved a bit.

Nelson Mandela was the topic I once fell out with Margaret Thatcher about. She never ceased to believe that Mandela was a terrorist. There was a string of Commonwealth conferences where the top item on the agenda was sanctions against South Africa. But Thatcher never supported them. She said to me,

'Chief Buthelezi doesn't believe there should be sanctions.' Chief Buthelezi was the leader of the KwaZulu Bantustan, one of the 'independent' territories, which at that time was widely seen as a puppet regime; Buthelezi willing to sell out Black South Africans for his own limited power. 'Prime Minister, that is more than a little patronising,' I replied, referring to the fact that she had found a Black man willing to argue her point for her. And she fixed me with one of her looks, and I knew I had irritated her.

We weren't in touch for several years after that. But then one day she came in to do the early evening news at ITN, and after I interviewed her I was sent back to ask if she would stick around for *News at Ten* too. I tried to explain that I was not currently in her graces, and that anyone other than me would likely have more luck. But I was the only journalist available, so I went down and asked. 'I will do it, Trevor,' she said, smiling. 'But only because it's you.'

Later on, when she was out of office, I went for a drink with her. I grew to admire and even became fond of her, though never a large swathe of her policies. But I did believe that she acted in good faith. She believed the things she said, and she believed they were the best route to prosperity for most people.

I had travelled the world a lot over those years, as I became the choice for what would become known as 'the big interview'. I have no real sense of why that was the case, other than I would put myself forward for such interviews, and no one else seemed to want to. I possessed very simple qualifications: I had always done the research and I was always on time. My father had drummed it into me that we should always be on time. To be otherwise was to tell someone that their time – that they themselves – didn't matter to you. And at the radio station, you couldn't be late for the race. You can't be late for a broadcast. I have known people who use lateness as a way of manifesting their power. They like to keep people hanging on, to show how busy and important they are. Much of my professional life has involved me being early to meetings and waiting for other people. Colonel Gaddafi was especially difficult. No one could tell him to turn up on time. So you'd make an arrangement with his people. No one was brave enough to tell him where and when he had to be, so you'd always end up waiting for hours.

I once spent several days following Colonel Gaddafi around Libya trying to interview him. I joined his convoy and watched as groups of villagers came out, beat drums, danced and chanted pro-government slogans. Gaddafi watched with a dull, vacant look that reminded me of a cow chewing. At one point he tried to wave his arms in time with their chants but couldn't quite get the rhythm right. The only time I saw him roused was when he drove a bulldozer through a customs post at the border with Tunisia. I was told we would spend a night in the desert with him, which I had to admit was not top of my list of things to do. The following morning I was waiting in his famous tent, where he would meet people. Out of the corner of my eye I watched as three guards with submachine guns crawled through the undergrowth. Then the man himself paused behind a rosebush, examined it, caressed it, took a deep draft of its fragrance, smiled and started to walk towards me. The only time he showed interest in our conversation was when he talked about British colonialism and he asked me if my island was finally free of it.

I went to the Philippines, Nicaragua and Lebanon. I was kicked out of Moscow for reporting Brezhnev's speech as 'long, rambling and self- serving'. I was once stopped in Uganda – at the exact moment I was being marched to jail – and asked for an autograph. I said, of course, as long as he was happy to call my producer and tell him it was looking highly likely I would miss cocktails at the British High Commission. I talked to mothers in Argentina whose children and husbands had been taken by the government, who would march in silent vigil. In Mozambique I saw starving people digging grass and roots out of riverbeds burned dry by drought. In Nicaragua, where I was reporting from just before the Sandinistas were swept from power, for some reason you could buy cigarettes and cigars, but matches were in such short supply that if you lit up outside the hotel a procession of smokers would hurtle towards you. One night, I got accidentally very drunk with a commander of the Sandinista Popular Army who told me that we people from the developing world should stick together. Then I was offered iguana for dinner, which he had shot himself.

I reported on the Reagan presidential campaign in 1980. Racing through the country, I would wake up in Galveston, Texas, or Savannah, Georgia. Reagan was a pure expression of a life lived away from politics. He possessed an entirely uncomplicated worldview based around a simple morality in which America and capitalism were right and communism was wrong. He stuck to big ideas, a simple vision. And the public adored it.

I also went to Pakistan for the first time, following the Russian invasion of Afghanistan. I followed drug-enforcement authorities in the north-west of Pakistan as they found enormous stores of dark brown heroin everywhere they looked.

Once, I was trying to interview Yasser Arafat, then chairman of the Palestinian Liberation Organisation. His people would call me up and say, 'He can see you this afternoon – in Morocco.' I would reply that I was not able to make it to Morocco that afternoon. They would harrumph as if this was a mutual diary issue, before proposing another date. A few weeks later, the same thing would occur. Eventually, I knew that he was appearing at a non-aligned conference in Harare. I called his people and they said they would find a slot for us to meet.

So, a few days later, I turned up at the airport in Zimbabwe and there were thirty heads of states. At the airport they asked for my accreditation, and I said I didn't have it yet. An official said, 'Go to the foreign office tomorrow.' I thought, 'I'm seeing him tomorrow, I won't bother with that.' The following morning Arafat's man came and picked me up from my hotel room. He drove me to the conference building. At the door was a guard with a rather large submachine gun. He asked for my accreditation. I explained I didn't have it. Arafat's man then said, 'This man has come from London to see the chairman and he's coming in with me.' The guard looked at us both and said, 'If he takes another step I will shoot him.' As we have already established by now, I am a great coward. I was trying to give the impression that nothing was further from my mind than to take another step forwards. 'You can't shoot this man. He is coming to see the chairman.' Then he dragged me past him. As we walked past, the guard jabbed the barrel of his gun into my stomach and locked eyes fiercely with me.

I got in eventually. My crew got in fine as they all had accreditation. We were setting up when Arafat arrived and we greeted each other. He apologised for the problems I had getting in. He sat down and we were literally about to roll when Robert Mugabe, the president of Zimbabwe, walked in and said, 'We've got a problem.' It transpired that there had been a mix-up and there was no one available to chair the next session. They needed Arafat to chair it. He assured me that he would be as quick as possible and hurried away. I was suddenly very aware that not only was I at the conference without accreditation, or my interviewee, I was in the highest security area. And there was a guard somewhere out there who was already gunning for me. After a couple of minutes, a harassed-looking aide came in and said they needed this meeting room for an emergency session and could we wait in the corridor. We demurred and went into the corridor. We were about twenty feet from the entrance, so I was desperate to keep a low profile.

At that point, the high commissioner of Zimbabwe walked past and said, 'Trevor! I didn't know you were here.' I tried to greet him quietly, explaining it was very last-minute and it was good to see him. Then General Zia-ul-Haq, the president of Pakistan, walked past, glanced at me, walked on a couple of paces, then walked back and boomed out, 'I know you! You have been to Pakistan to interview me!' I nodded and greeted him. Then the aide who had moved us out into the corridor said, 'You're going to have to move down. Three of the delegates need to have a meeting, and this is the only free space.' So we shuffled down as far into the corner of the corridor as we could. Out came Fidel Castro, Colonel Gaddafi, Samora Machel, the president of Mozambique and Thomas Sankara, the president of Burkina Faso. We were about ten feet from them. They were having what was clearly an intense conversation and we were pressed as far away from them as we possibly could be, trying to project an impression of nonchalance, that we were in no way trying to listen in. Any minute, I was thinking, that guard is going to appear and make good on his promise. This situation lasted for two hours; two hours in which I imagined the barrel of a gun pressed into my side. We did the interview with Yasser Arafat. Perhaps because of the context, I tried to press him on some issues but didn't feel like I was very successful. At one point, though, I asked him what the PLO had achieved after all these years, and he said, 'At the beginning, Palestinians were just numbers. Now we are a cause.' But the rest of the time it felt rather cagey.

When the interview finished, Arafat apologised for keeping me waiting and said he would put us up at a hotel, that his aide would arrange it. Then he was gone. The aide came over and I explained that, although it was a generous offer, I had already arranged to stay with friends that night. This was a lie, but I just needed to go and lie down on my own in my hotel. The aide explained that he couldn't go against the chairman's wishes. He looked rather worried about the whole thing. I understood that he needed to perform the duties of a good host. So instead, I suggested that perhaps he could buy us a round at the bar on behalf of the chairman and that would be enough. There I had the biggest whisky, and for the first time in about three hours my hands stopped shaking. The same rules applied as when I had been interviewing people for Radio Trinidad. People, most people at least, have a great desire to talk and explain themselves. To have their side of things put forwards. The journalist's job is to ask questions with just the right amount of give and just the right amount of bite in them; to open up a space where they leave the safety of the utterly prepared remark and are encouraged to operate somewhere a little more dangerous.

I travelled the world, and when I could I returned home. I called my parents whenever I was able to. But I was in Moscow the day my father died. I was working for Channel 4, having set up some interviews, when the message came in that my father had died. I popped into the Kremlin and apologised that I would be unable to do the interviews because I was on my way back to Trinidad via London. But the official told me to come in and sit down and tell him about my father. He poured me a large glass of very good vodka, and I told him about this man. About what it had been like to grow up with him. And, as it was happening, I wondered what my father would have thought of his name being spoken of in the Kremlin.

It is not uncommon when you lose a parent to be full of the things you didn't say to them. I thought of the time he had come to visit me in London and we went and stood across the Thames from the Houses of Parliament. A school trip pulled up in their coach near me, and one child recognised me and started knocking on the window and waving, so I waved back. Then there were two, and then more. And quite soon the children were all streaming out of the bus for me to autograph things for them to take back home. I wasn't entirely sure my father knew what autographs were, but he stood about ten yards away, watching me talking to the children, watching them excited, laughing and smiling, asking me questions and giving me things out of their school bags to write my name on. And I got a strong sense that he must have known that whatever I was doing it couldn't have been entirely bad. Afterwards, we didn't talk about what had happened. But he had a smile on his face. I am glad we got to share that moment together.

I only hope he knew how grateful I am that he was my father.

9

Last Man Standing

Australia versus West Indies, Fourth Test, 1993

'You're Trevor McDonald!'

I nodded, slightly saddened at the now-decreasing frequency of people confusing me for Clive Lloyd. I shook his hand. I hoped I had learned a little more about wine since my offer to John Arlott had failed to meet his standard all those years before, but my tastes still hovered more naturally at the cheaper and more cheerful end of the spectrum. As the delivery driver began to bring the cases of wine in, I had a decorator painting the hall, who stopped work to watch the boxes stack up. After the eighth was placed in the hall, he caught the delivery driver's eye and said, 'Blimey, all this on half an hour's work a night!'

It was 1992 and I had recently been made the single news anchor for *News at Ten* – a fact that I had still not really got used to. If I was honest, when I'd heard that I was to be a single anchor, I'd been preparing myself for what I would do when I had to go elsewhere for a job. But there had been some sort of audience research, and whatever qualities a television viewer decides a news anchor requires, they had decided I possessed enough of them. In many ways it was utterly bizarre. Was it vocal rhythm? Was it facial expression? Eye contact? I like to think that the seriousness with which I took the role of reading the news somehow communicated itself to those watching. I fundamentally believe that without the free flow of good quality information, the engine of democracy seizes up entirely. So I saw the job of the newsreader as primarily making sure the most people were most likely to know about the most important events; that someone focused on living their own life, looking after their family, to whom events around the world might seem distant and somehow unimportant, would be grabbed by them. *News at Ten* had been from its inception an act of faith in the British public's capacity for news. It was the first thirty-minute news bulletin in the country. At first it had only been scheduled for a trial run of thirteen weeks, and there were certainly those who felt it would not fly. But it became hugely popular and quickly became part of the nation's routine. They told me, almost apologetically, 'It will be five nights a week' – as if this was some onerous hardship; I would have done it six nights a week, and on Sundays too – never in my life had I thought I would get that opportunity. There was no way that I wasn't going to put my all into it.

I always wanted to find the point of connection in a news story. Because I genuinely believe that a functioning media, one that tells us stories about each other, is the best way of helping us imagine what others go through. One of the reasons I have always loved to read books is because they transport you into another place and time, a kind of direct connection to the thoughts of people distant from you by hundreds of years and thousands of miles. Reading books is a direct invitation to empathy. But it is also a mechanism for holding those with power to account. I worked terribly, terribly hard to try to make the telling of those stories as accessible as possible. In the back of the car ITN would organise to drive me home after reading the news, I would use my time to call up my Washington contacts, who would be just winding down their working days and keen to discuss what was going on there. So I'd spend the drive home talking to them. I was always hugely aware that my line of work was not, in the grand scheme of things, hard graft. It wasn't like working at an oil refinery, doing odd jobs, making shoes – that was hard work. Sitting in a car asking questions so that later you could ask better questions was clearly a blessed professional life. I once heard from one of my US contacts that there were some disgruntled staff who hadn't been invited to a formal event at Buckingham Palace. So I got their names and offered to take all five of them out for a swanky meal in Knightsbridge. We ate and drank till midnight and, from that day onwards, I'd multiplied my contacts in the White House. Was that partly cynical? Possibly. But I also felt bad for them. I heard my mother and father's voices: how you should always entertain guests; how you should show people respect. And that's how I ended up getting an interview with George Bush at the White House when these things were gripped tightly. I have never overly valued my time: not because I see it has no value, but because I understood that I could squeeze my time and get a result. I applied the same technique when trying to call Colin Powell's office to arrange an interview and kept getting no reply. I convinced my editor that the thing to do was to go and ask for an appointment in person. I'd fly in on the red-eye, wait till I could see who I needed to see, request an interview, and then fly straight back. And when I saw the person whose job it was to gatekeep Powell's time, he said, 'You came all the way from England just to see us?' I said yes, and he said that there'd be a chance to meet next week. We had a Washington correspondent who told me it was strange that Powell had agreed to meet me, as they'd been writing to him for several years. I understood the idea that you had to work, to signal work, to signal respect. I'm not sure it was conscious. It was just what I had seen and what I had absorbed. I am what my parents showed me, what they taught me.

In 1990 I'd spent every morning for a month at the Iraqi Cultural Centre in Tottenham Court Road. I had got to know the young Iraqi diplomat there. At first he was suspicious because there had been protests at the invasion of Kuwait, but I would hammer away until he came to the door. Then he would serve me thick Iraqi coffee that made my heart pound as he told me that he would, yet again, send a Telex to Baghdad. That he had been assured the only interview would be with me at ITN. The interview I was after was, of course, Saddam Hussein. He was a subject of fascination and horror after he'd broken his word and invaded Kuwait, set fire to their oilfields and detained hundreds of hostages. His threat to make the deserts run with rivers of American blood had certainly got people's attention. Every pronouncement was scanned for what it might mean, for what his next move might be.

I had resigned myself to waiting indefinitely, when the

phone rang one weekend. It was my friend from the cultural centre. He told me Baghdad would like me there as soon as possible. It had proved to be a long and bizarre process, complicated by the difficulty of working through the impenetrable layers of Middle Eastern politics and bureaucracy. At times it was like trying to grasp a mirage. It went on for months. But when I mentioned a visa to my friend from the cultural centre, he told me he did the visas and one would be ready for me to collect on Monday.

In Baghdad, no one could confirm if the interview was going to happen at all. They certainly couldn't say when. Over the next few days, I would go to the media relations people in the morning, they would suck their teeth in the manner of a sceptical garage attendant and say we'd have to come back in the afternoon. In the afternoon, the same performance – followed by an instruction to return the next morning. It was intimated that the BBC were not happy that we had got the interview and were furiously doing everything they could to eject us. After a few days of this I was summoned to a government building and felt sure that this must mean something was happening. But it turned out this was just to say hello to the staff who had done their degrees at British universities and knew who I was. A similarly urgent invitation was received, to have dinner.

Then, suddenly, the next day, the whole team was invited to attend a meeting to discuss how the interview would be shot and who would do the translation. Our answers were meticulously written down. Yet there was still no definitive answer on whether the interview would happen, never mind when.

But the following morning we were told to return to our hotel and not leave. I couldn't dismiss the idea that this could be a very soft form of kidnap. Several hours later the phone rang and they told me to pack an overnight bag. As I paced my hotel room, I thought again about the many conversations we'd had in London regarding how to approach this interview. The one thing we were all in total alignment about was that it had to appear tough. There had been some debate about whether it was morally right to interview Saddam Hussein at all. I felt strongly that it was, but only if we were seen to be pushing him as hard as we could. There was certainly no point bowling underarm. But he had a terrifying reputation. One of my colleagues decided to recount to me the story of the time Saddam had been holding a governmental meeting and someone had pushed too hard. He took them outside, shot them in the head, then went back in and continued the meeting, which I assume proceeded swiftly from that point onwards. I was terrified, but only on a professional level. It was a big coup for ITN and I was aware that both ITN's and my reputation were at stake.

Things hadn't been helped when I'd run my proposed first question past the British ambassador in Baghdad, Harold Walker: 'Mr President, is it in the tradition of Arab hospitality to invade and rape a neighbouring country?' The ambassador almost fell off his chair. Then he laughed. Then he went pale and said, 'Please don't tell me you're serious.'

Around 5 p.m. that afternoon a convoy of Iraqi army cars arrived to pick up my camera crew, my ITN producer Angela Frier and me. After a few minutes on the road, I realised that the driver had no idea where we were going. At every turning or roundabout, he would be given an instruction at the last possible moment and have to wrench the wheel. Eventually we arrived at a guesthouse and were told to wait for further instructions.

A very nice man in a suit greeted us at the guesthouse and said, 'Welcome. What would you like for breakfast?' I assumed that he didn't know English very well and said, 'Don't you mean dinner?' He said, 'No, breakfast.' And that's how we learned that we were staying the night. I couldn't help but feel nervous that we were in the middle of nowhere, that apparently the phones couldn't make calls outwards, and nobody seemed to know anything about the interview. We spent the night there, and most of the next day, pacing around the rooms of the presidential guesthouse. At dinner one of the information officers who had been to university in London took me through all of the places he missed dearly in the city. But when I asked about the interview, he just became quiet and smiled. This pattern repeated the next day. Then at about six o'clock that evening, suddenly the stillness of the house was disturbed. We were told to be ready to leave in five minutes. We were also told to leave our camera equipment, as alternative equipment would be provided. This was incredibly annoying, but we had to say yes.

Again we set off in a convoy of cars, but it was slow going as we had to stop for the lead car to tell us all where we were going. Only the very most senior inner team could know where we were going.

We arrived at a building surrounded by soldiers just as the sun was setting. We passed through metal detectors and were patted down. They took everything: my watch, my jewellery and the book with my notes for the interview. Then we were driven away to the presidential palace for another set of searches. They took our shoes. Then we were sat in a high-ceilinged room with a swirling gold and yellow carpet and enormous deep armchairs. The equipment was already set up, and although there were numerous small technical problems, my team set about fixing them. They brought back our shoes.

At one point the translator asked if there were any 'unfamiliar words' in any of my questions. We had made it a point of principle not to supply a list of questions beforehand. So I said that there was only one: 'disembowelling'. He swallowed. Frowned. Why might we be using that word, he enquired? I explained that there had been reports of pregnant women being disembowelled by Iraqi troops in Kuwait. He adjusted his glasses and thanked me for letting him know.

Then, almost three hours after we'd left the guesthouse, President Saddam Hussein entered the room, surrounded by a vast array of men in dark suits with bulging armpits. Then there were interpreters, cabinet ministers and a bunch of technicians. The first thing he did was have us pose with him for a photograph. Then, as the crew sorted out microphones, I studied him. He was a big man, with large hands. But he seemed thoughtful and serious. Then it was time for the first ball. At the words 'invade and rape' his ministers audibly winced and rocked back in their seats. He feigned amusement and asked if it was an English thing to do. And so we were off. Me trying to find the right pace and line. Him playing most things with a straight bat.

When the interview ended, the president got up and said he wanted to have a word with me. My fear returned. I had never felt in any personal danger, but I thought he was about to say that my questions had been irreverent. Instead, he lectured me for twenty minutes on what awful people the Kuwaitis were. Unable to see the firestorm gathering over his country, he was obsessed by Kuwait's wealth.

As we drove back, I reflected that I was not sure the interview had accomplished much. Though no one could say it was a soft interview – the questions had decent line and length – he just hadn't really swung for anything. There had been five or six of his cabinet ministers around. At one point they were crowding around, and I could see them constantly in my peripheral vision. I said to one of them, 'Look here, can you back off a bit?' And he replied, 'You don't understand. We never see him asked questions that he has to answer.'

As ever, once the interview was over there was adrenaline. When I got back to my room, there were five members of his PR team who wanted to know what it had been like. As we continued to drink the bottle of my whisky they had found, I started to tell them how the interview had gone. But I realised that what they actually meant was, 'What was he like?' Saddam Hussein was kept so distant from all but the very inner circle; they'd worked for him for fifteen years but they'd never been near him. They wanted to know what he was wearing, how he behaved. I realised then that much like Gaddafi all those years before, part of the business of being a dictator was being kept separate from your people.

Several weeks later it took forty-three days to pummel the Iraqi defences into submission. Within a hundred more hours the Iraqi army was defeated.

I was working so much during that period that cricket

functioned as a kind of relaxant: a familiar rhythm. It helped that West Indian excellence had become almost routine. There had been the 1984 tour of England, which became known as 'the blackwash', because we had won 5–0. Joel Garner was in astonishing form and was joined by Malcolm Marshall, the Barbadian. By now, it was common for fans of other cricketing nations to exclaim at the laboratory that we grew these bowlers in. Marshall was a little different in that he was shorter than many of his elite fast-bowling brethren at only 5 foot 10. However, the pace he generated was astonishing. Michael Holding watched, flummoxed, early on as Marshall walked around with weights strapped to his legs to increase their strength. He hardly seemed to stop when he reached the crease, open-chested but with soft hands that knew exactly how to control the ball. He had a vicious steep bouncer, and a 'skiddy' saw numerous batsmen bemusedly out as the ball bounced at leg and cut back. He had it all. Throughout the eighties he would go on to be statistically the best Test bowler in the world.

The 1984 tour also saw Gordon Greenidge bat for the ages. Although it's hard to believe, he wasn't really in good form coming into the second Test at Lord's. In the first Test he'd been out for 19, and in the first innings of the second caught for 1. England had declared early on the fifth day, leaving a target of 342. The pitch suited the batters, but they would require around a run a minute – 66.1 overs later they reached it. Gordon Greenidge at his deadliest saw the ball as well as he ever would. He was all sinewy grace, the ball snapping from his bat. It felt like he had utter control of where the ball went, down to the inch. Here, again, the flame he nurtured inside himself from his miserable childhood as a West Indian immigrant in Reading seemed to burn brightly, powering his shots with retributive force as he reached 214 not out. The power and the fury. The following season the West Indies welcomed England on tour and beat them again 5–0.

We also had an astonishing record against Australia over that period, which included the fiery tour of the Caribbean by Australia in 1991. A bad tempered one-day series before the Test matches saw the West Indies accused of intimidating umpires and possessing 'brittle' batting. Australian captain Bobby Simpson also used the term 'professional fouls' to describe the slow over rates. Viv Richards was interviewed and said that Simpson and other players were 'shouting their mouths off'. He added that Simpson was a 'moaner and a bad loser', before concluding, 'Bobby Simpson ain't our cup of tea at all.'

The two teams had form. The Australians were a loud, abrasive bunch, who used every strategy to get into their opponents' heads. In the first Test, amid long rain delays, an uninspiring draw saw the West Indies selectors worried enough that they informed Viv Richards of their plans to drop Gordon Greenidge, Malcolm Marshall and Jeff Dujon. Viv suggested they might like to not do this.

In the second Test, in Guyana, Richards saw a much-improved batting performance and some brilliant borderline murderous bowling from Marshall, who took 3 wickets (Dujon 7 catches). Greenidge's numbers though read 2 then 5. All the talk was of the sad demise of a once great batsman. The West Indies won by 10 wickets, but when Dean Jones went to congratulate Viv Richards he gave him short shrift, later saying, 'You don't expect him to come over and say, "How are you doing? You want a Tooheys?" You don't do things like that. When I draw the sword, I draw the sword. When I draw it, that's it.'

This, to me, was the great difference between the cricket that grew in West Indian soil and that of Australian soil. Respect was a non-negotiable part of our game. It was much more optional in theirs, and if it needed to be temporarily suspended for victory? Well, so be it.

The third Test in Trinidad was again ruined by rain and resulted in a draw. On to Bridgetown for the fourth. Here, less than 20 miles away from where he'd been born almost forty years earlier, the consensus was that Greenidge was over the hill. Things began in distemper: Greenidge out for 10, but the whole side seeming to wilt under the abrasive Australian bowling. At one point Desmond Haynes and Ian Healy, the Australian wicketkeeper, promised extensive and future violence to each other for a very long time. The West Indies were 149 all out. There was always the hope that a pitch so supportive of bowlers might offer some to ours as well as theirs. And so it went as Curtly Ambrose, Courtney Walsh and Marshall took 9 wickets and sent two of the batters to seek medical attention as Australia were all out for 134.

And so, on a pitch that seemed to be becoming utterly un-predictable, out stepped the now veteran Gordon Greenidge: the island of his birth set to witness at close hand the in-glorious end of a career defined by flashes of self-contained brilliance. There he stood, waiting to face the new ball. I cannot conceive of how it is done with every muscle fibre, every neuron, ever sinew in perfect condition. To stand there at almost forty, on that pitch . . . it was an act of bravery.

But when the first ball came, Greenidge struck it sweetly to square-leg. As the balls came, he didn't force it, he played where he needed to. At 30, there was a glorious thumping drive through extra cover. Gradually he settled in. There it was: that old ice-cold fury. Slowly, the shots came to have the inevitability of revenge. His shot selection was, for that time, perfect. If it wasn't on, it wasn't on. If it was, it would be punished. He reached 50 and barely raised his bat. The shots kept coming – one drive saw a fielder hit the hoarding with an audible thump as he forlornly chased it. The day finished with him at 85 not out.

The next day, Richie Richardson took on the role of driving the batting, leaving Greenidge to protect what he had. At 93 a missed boundary saw the bowler say something he didn't like and Greenidge pointed at him. He reached 100 but still with barely any acknowledgement. His captain came to embrace him and received barely a touch of the gloves. The runs kept coming, the second new ball barely making a difference. As he approached 150 Greenidge began to improvise, playing at one point a kind of spinning shot to square-leg that had looked like a pull until the last fraction of a second when the ball hit his straight bat. He was hitting the ball harder now, as if accelerating towards a finish line. At 150 he waved his bat for the first time. The crowd howled in joy. He kept going, hefting the ball to the boundary until his double century came up. There, after 402 balls and the best part of ten hours, he pointed to Viv Richards, who had kept faith in him. He was out for 226. As he left the field, he waved his bat to all sides of the ground. When Australia were all out for 208, The West Indies had won by 343 runs.

This ability to find what it took to avoid defeat became almost routine. Between 1980 and 1995 we would win five consecutive Frank Worrell trophies and draw only one, as part of a record of twenty-nine Test series without a loss. But in January 1993 on tour in Australia we came as close as we ever did.

It was a tour where I could not help but begin by lamenting, a little, what we had lost. Viv Richards had retired in 1991, as had Greenidge. Malcolm Marshall went a year later. We still had a team full of astonishing talent. Of course, there was the rookie Brian Lara. His record speaks for itself. His bat speed was remarkable, his power and precision thrilling. He seemed to be able to pick where to place his shots at will. But perhaps, like pop music, it is only truly possible to feel love for cricketers at a certain stage in one's life? Lara was a batter I admired, but following on from Clive Lloyd and Viv Richards, his captaincy would always feel like it was missing a certain ineffable quality to me. But I'm aware that a lot of men of a certain age have looked out over a cricket pitch and said the same thing.

Our bowlers at this time were Ian Bishop and Curtly Ambrose, Courtney Walsh and Kenny Benjamin. Bishop had been one of the fastest bowlers in the world until successive back injuries forced him to rebuild his action. One of his balls hit the debutant Justin Langer in the back of the head and his legs went like a boxer's.

Curtly Ambrose was one of the most controlled pure pace bowlers you would ever see. His ability to get movement and accuracy alongside the pace was just superb. But the power was remarkable. Batsmen who faced him likened it to staring down a charging bull.

Courtney Walsh had a metronomic quality. He was quick, sure, but it was the regulation of his bowls, his ability to just keep putting a batsman under pressure, that wore them down.

The first Test in Brisbane was a draw. The second in Melbourne saw a Shane Warne masterclass of 7 for 52 win a 1–0 lead. In the third Test in Sydney, Brian Lara scored 277 to announce himself to the world. With that exaggerated, over-stated backlift, he just seemed to have an extra half-second and played the ball on the rise. Anything at all short was sent for the boundary. There were laser-guided cover-drives, cuts and hooks. It was balletic. But rain regularly stopped play: a draw. So it was on to Adelaide for the fourth Test with all to play for.

We batted first but were bowled out within 68 overs for 252. Brian Lara made 52 but Merv Hughes and his aston-ishing handlebar moustache, which he was rumoured to insure for £200,000, took 5 for 64. Before light stopped play, Australia were 3 for 1. The second day lost almost four hours to rain but saw Australia reach 100 for 3. David Boon was forced to retire after he took an Ambrose ball to the elbow.

On the third day the rain cleared and Ambrose took con-trol. He tore through the Australian middle order to take 6 for 74: ball after ball, perfect length, brilliant direction. The word that sprung to mind was 'control'. This was fast bowling, not as physical expression but a tactical decision as they were all out for 213. Tim May, the Australian off-spinner, was in-censed at being given caught out from a Walsh bouncer that he would later say had left a big red stain on his shirt. But he got his revenge that afternoon, as he took 5 for 9 and the West Indies fell apart, all out for 146.

Australia had a target of 186 to win the match. The West Indian attack was brutal as they got Australia to 102 for 8. Justin Langer, who had been hit in that first innings, took four bouncers to the helmet. But he stood upright somehow. He and Tim May made an admirable, dogged partnership of 42 before Langer was caught out at mid-wicket. Craig McDermott was number 11 and Australia needed 42 runs to win. I never normally let myself get carried away but even I began to feel this victory was surely a matter of 'when' not 'if'.

The plan was clearly to ruffle their feathers and they both certainly faced their share of short balls. But in that quintessentially Australian way they refused to back down. The ball went past the edge numerous times but we couldn't get a nick, and all the time Australia were edging the scoreboard along. You could see a tightness coming into the West Indies as the realisation that they might lose began to dawn.

And then suddenly Australia needed two runs to win. Walsh delivered and McDermott hit into the leg-side. Desmond Haynes managed to lunge and get enough on the ball to stop it dead. No run.

A couple of balls blocked but then Walsh bowled a short one and, as McDermott turned and tried to get out of the way, the ball flicked off something as it went through to the wicket-keeper. There was celebration and a pause before the umpire's finger went up. To this day McDermott maintains the ball hit the grille of his helmet. But at the time the Australian players, and definitely the West Indian players, were certain he'd hit it with bat or glove. There was delirium on the pitch and in the stands. The West Indies had won by one run.

At the final Test in Perth, Ambrose would take 7 for 25 as the West Indies won the Test by an innings and 25 runs and the series 2–1.

But it was that fourth Test, won by the smallest margin of runs in Test history, that burns brightest all these years later.

10

The End of an Era

Australia versus West Indies, 1996

'Good evening. Few if any events will touch the lives of so many of us as the death of Princess Diana.' I sat, looking out at the camera, aware as perhaps never before that I was looking out of the televisions of millions of people. Her death was perhaps the most astonishing thing I've ever witnessed in Britain. I remember when I first saw the bank of flowers at Kensington Palace. It was waist-height by this point. The crowds of people, many of them crying. The two boys walking along behind the car. It was a moment when the public and the private collapsed into one; a moment in which someone was both one of the most famous people in the world but also a mother who died far too young. We were utterly determined to make the coverage the very best it could be. I stayed in a hotel near ITN for a week because the coverage was constant. We had enormous teams working every hour to make sure there was no aspect not covered.

We now know the tension behind the scenes regarding how the royal family should be seen to respond. That role, which is to never show emotion, to never be ruffled, to be that constant point of reference that they believed the country required. But the Queen came, to look at the flowers, to read the cards, to take flowers and lay them. There were (and continue to be) people who viewed it as a sort of collective hysteria.

I had met Diana a few times and very much liked her. She was very easy to talk to. The joke of a conversation with a traditional royal was: they'd say, 'A plumber? How interesting, you must have seen a great many pipes.' And then they'd move on. But Diana had that genuine quality of curiosity. I remember once she came to lunch at ITN and somebody talked about the fact that one of our colleagues was a trainspotter. Diana had never heard of trainspotters. 'What do you mean? You just go around looking for trains?' she said, and she couldn't stop laughing. She found causes that she believed in and she drew attention to them. She didn't have to do that. When she shook hands with and embraced an HIV positive patient, that was a powerful moment in removing stigma.

In many ways, her death still feels so powerful because it occurred just before the internet and the way social media refashioned how we would experience news for ever. Back in August 1997 there were still four main channels (Channel 5 having begun a few months earlier but still not really part of most people's televisual diet). For many people those peals of a bell punctuating the headlines take people immediately back to that era. There was no Twitter (or X) then, no smartphones. Many people woke up on Sunday morning and heard the news for the first time. Mothers called upstairs to children, families sat around the television in their pyjamas. There was no citizen journalism, very few eyewitness accounts, no shaky handheld footage from a phone. It was one of the last global news events where that was the case.

And in Britain it held a special charge because of our peculiar relationship with the royal family. Growing up, we had been raised to be broadly pro monarchy without even thinking about it. In Trinidad we were kept keen with regular visits of various members of the family. I remember once, in secondary school, Princess Margaret was scheduled to appear. We were all made to line up in the morning sun, which was already pretty fierce. We stood there for an hour in the sun while we waited for the motorcade that finally arrived, at which point the car slowed down almost imperceptibly and a gloved hand emerged and waved. I do remember wondering if it was worth one of our number fainting in the heat for. But I would never have voiced such an opinion.

Now, I look back on it and wonder what the thinking was behind our lining up to watch Princess Margaret's car drive by. There were calypsos written about her marriage. At the end of a film screening in the cinema, the national anthem would play and people would stand to attention. Later, as the mood on the island swung towards more rampant nationalism, and there were more and more people scrambling to leave, fewer and fewer stood to attention. Professionally, I had not a huge amount to do with the royal family, but I knew people that did. I heard the story of someone who was spending an evening with Princess Margaret. They were all rather merry, several cocktails in, and felt things were informal enough to enquire after her sister. She replied icily, the alcohol almost visibly evaporating from her bloodstream, 'You mean Her Majesty the Queen?'

I met the Queen many times, and found her as witty and sharp as everyone always said she was. I was once doing a documentary on her and the Commonwealth in the Bahamas. There were demonstrations at the docks by the royal yacht. We were delayed trying to avoid them and so were late to the reception. I apologised profusely to the Queen when I arrived. And she replied, with a wicked glint in her eye, 'Ah, yes, the protests. I think my particular favourite banner was "Our Chief's a thief".' I also showed her around the new ITN studios when they opened and she was wearing a dress that was the exact shade that disappeared in front of the green-screen technology that ITN were very proud of. Though I don't think footage of it exists, the Queen would just have been a head floating through the studio.

I remember when the Obamas went to see the Queen. They were overwhelmed by the glitter and gold. They had brought her a small, modest gift to say thank you, a small brooch. They felt a little embarrassed by that once surrounded by the glitz of Buckingham Palace. But when the Queen returned to the ambassador's house in Washington, she was wearing that brooch.

I once asked a Commonwealth leader, 'What does the Queen actually do at the Commonwealth conferences?' 'She is there,' he replied. 'She has a massive knowledge about those Commonwealth countries. She shows that it matters to her.' She genuinely believed in the duty of her role. How she must be seen.

I interviewed Prince Charles about the Prince's Trust, once, and very much admired his work. I also have a lot of time for Prince William. We did a programme on the Windrush generation and, as part of that, he went to Yorkshire and met up with a man called Alford Gardner, who had come to Britain in 1948 and set up the first Caribbean cricket club. Prince William arrived at his home in Leeds and took him to Headingley Cricket Ground for a party. He made sure to spend time talking to Alford, to communicate how important he and his generation were to Britain. Alford bowled a ball at the future King of England. There will be those who roll their eyes at this, but it is impossible to convey what that will have felt like to someone from Alford's background.

Over the years, I have never lost my horror for violence. I remember talks collapsing at a summit in Geneva just before the Iraq war. I was in Saudi Arabia that day and wandered around an airbase where we were filming at the time. I saw some of my colleagues snap straight into a professional reaction, thinking about how they would report matters. But I was still so caught up in that first moment, the sequence of events that those talks collapsing would inevitably set in motion. There would be deaths in their hundreds of thousands. Those events at that summit would now destroy so many people's lives for generations. But I knew it was important to broadcast. It was part of the job: we showed people what was going on. You didn't get to look away. You had to go where the stories were. I thought it was important for people to know about what was going on. Perhaps if we could continue to show the impact of these things on everyday people, you could educate people about what such decisions actually meant in real terms. It was important to try to show how we were bound together as human beings.

I worked almost the entirety of my career in a media environment that is now almost unrecognisable. There were few enough TV channels (you could count them on one hand). Newspapers were booming. It felt as if the mechanisms for our culture to examine itself were many and varied, but there was a sense somehow of looking at the same thing. People would watch the same television programmes, at the same time, then they would talk about them together the next day. Today we live in a landscape that is fractured beyond recognition. And part of what has been fractured is the general faith in the central endeavour of journalism. In the US there are entirely discrete news bubbles. The right-wing news has entire stories that don't exist on the other networks. They function not as media organisations but as propaganda outlets. They have lost that sense of mission, to try to find, to the best of your imperfect human efforts, something that strives for the quality of truth. But at ITN I felt I was close to the centre of that process.

I can honestly say I never felt ambitious. Someone once went back and told my mother and father that, as far as he could see, I was running the whole of British television. What I felt was that I had to work hard. Nothing was going to come easily. Ambition speaks to that sense of thinking several steps ahead. I was head down in the furrow, concentrating on the desire not to fail in that moment. That does, of course, generate momentum, but you may not realise it from the depths of the furrow.

This was a period where the dominance of the West Indies over all comers began to come to an end. And nowhere was that more evident than against the old enemy, the Australians.

It had been noticeable in the spring of 1995 when the Waugh brothers at bat and Paul Reiffel and Shane Warne with ball had led to an epoch-ending 2–1 loss. Then, in the World Cup semi-final in 1996, the West Indies looked all set to win before crumbling from 165 for 2 to 202 all out, a defeat later blamed on the strategy of holding back the specialist batters. Even when they needed 35 from 39 balls, Ottis Gibson came out and was almost immediately caught. Under the pressure of scoring the requisite runs, the batsmen seemed to crumble; even a remarkable six from Richie Richardson could not save them. The West Indies needed 10 from the last over. The innings ended with the unedifying sight of Walsh, helmetless, refusing to try to get Richardson back on strike and instead going for the ungainly slog of all slogs only to be bowled by Damien Fleming's off-cutter.

The final indignity was listening to Tony Greig say, 'The Aussies have sneaked in and won a great game of cricket.' After a group stage that had seen us lose to Kenya, Richie Richardson resigned as captain and Wes Hall and Andy Roberts were sacked as manager and coach.

Several months later, we had lost the Test series to Australia 3–2, and the seemingly never-ending series of autopsies would really begin.

As a West Indian cricket fan I have been asked frequently what went wrong with West Indian cricket. There are two answers: one simple and one not so simple. One answer is to flip it and say that the sustained excellence of a tiny collection of disparate islands in the seventies, eighties and first half of the nineties was one of the greatest sporting lightning strikes ever. What has happened subsequently is nothing more than a very visible reversion to the mean. After all, one does not criticise Leicester City for all the seasons they have failed since they last won the league.

Everyone has a theory: from poorly managed resources and incompetent administrators to a generation of youth more interested in basketball than cricket. What is certainly true is that the miracle of sustained West Indian success, which seemed at one point to occur naturally, has stopped happening. A simple explanation is that richer countries have regained the advantage they lost for a generation through the application of money. They kept to a standard that a poorer region was able to impose but not maintain. And these days, in a global game where there are more and more places to watch and play cricket, that is a gap that is harder and harder to close.

Not having a professional domestic game in the islands was always an issue, but now there is so much top-class cricket to be sampled globally, a sub-par domestic game is fatal. That means that talent is thin at every stage of the ecosystem. In many ways it is a predictable phase. As that old gravity of colonialism fades, perhaps the sport introduced by its adherents simply means less. If the seventies and eighties saw the fullest expression of cricket wielded as a weapon, perhaps subsequent generations see less need to wield that weapon.

So many of the islands have been suffering economically. Globalisation has not been kind. The long legacy of being a single-crop larder for various empires means that the island economies are especially vulnerable to price fluctuations in sugar or bananas. Some of the smaller islands have taken to selling citizenship to raise funds, which contributes a not inconsiderable amount of money to their economies. The irony is that these islands – whose labour force was populated by the non-people of slave labour, and then indentured servitude, to remove economic value wholesale from the islands – are now using their status as independent nations to generate revenue.

In this context, it goes without saying that there is much more chance of leaving the islands through a place at an American university with a basketball or athletics scholarship than through cricket. Cricket used to be the only ticket out, now it just isn't. And if all of this happens at the same time, it is hard to make an argument for investing in a sport whose popularity is waning – even if one reason for that may be the shoddy surroundings and support. Lara spent so many years of his captaincy battling against what he saw as institutional failings. The first time the World Cup was held in the West Indies was 2007, in spite of the fact we had seen such success at this competition. I happened to be on the island of Grenada just before the competition was due to start. There had been a fierce hurricane called Ivan months before, and on the hills you could still see the ruins of houses and shacks that had been flattened by the winds. It had uprooted trees, pulled down power lines. I asked my taxi driver to take me past the cricket ground, expecting to see similar evidence of damage. But it was spotless. When I asked how this had managed to escape any damage at all, he told me, 'They made sure it was built by the Chinese. They built special foundations to make sure it would bend but not break.'

As ever, of course, we must be careful to differentiate between cricket and Test cricket, not least because there are shoots of green in the shorter forms of the game. Since 2008 West Indian cricketers have thrived in the Indian Premier League. For those for whom the sheer heft of Test cricket is the point, this may offer cold comfort, but I have a lot of time for those who see an ongoing opportunity to make the game fit the lives of those in full-time employment. To be a fan of cricket who has a job when there is a Test match on is to be transformed into a naughty school child sneaking off to find out the score, or hunching at your desk with earphones in. I remember the lamentations when Kerry Packer came into the game. There is always a feeling that making cricket easier to play or view is somehow betraying its soul. But I also have sympathy for the view that anything that increases working folk's ability to see the game is a good thing. For me, the bombast of Twenty20 is a little much. Like a rich dessert, I'm not sure I could do it with every meal. There is great lamentation over the shorter forms of cricket and attempts to work out where the soul of cricket resides, so that it can be protected. But I am old enough to remember when having four fast bowlers was seen as tantamount to betraying the spirit of cricket. Not long before that it was a game that could not be played by the majority of the population on the island I grew up on. I believe in cricket's ability to bend and not break.

11

Looking Forwards

'Tonight, more than two hundred years after a former colony won the right to determine its own destiny, the task of perfecting our union moves forward.' November 2012, and my reaction to the news that Obama had won a second term was a much less polite version of, 'Thank heavens for that.'

Just under four years earlier, I had been in Washington for Obama's inauguration, rising before dawn to watch the crowds assemble in the freezing morning to make sure they got a good spot. The air was so cold it burned your face. But they came, streaming to find a place. By late morning it was the largest crowd ever assembled in Washington. I remembered the look in her eye when my mother had talked about segregation in America. 'What I would give for her to be alive to see this,' I thought. As the day progressed, seeing men and women in tears, unable to process what they were witnessing, was commonplace. 'It's too much,' I remember one woman calling out. 'It's just too much.'

I'd followed the campaign trail for Ronald Reagan in 1980, and then reported on George Bush Senior in 1988. I watched the Reverend Jesse Jackson as he reminded Black Americans that 'the hands that once picked cotton can now pick a president'. I had watched as, unable to ally his rhetorical power to the patient power-building of governance, Jackson had not been able to make good on that promise. But now an African American was about to enter the White House, a house built by enslaved people.

Just over six months later, during a portion of the president's speech that was dealing with healthcare reform and immigrants, Joe Wilson, the Republican representative for South Carolina shouted out, 'You lie.' It was from South Carolina, of course, that Robert Rhett, the dean of the Fire-Eaters, a pro-slavery group who sought to revive America's involvement in the Atlantic slave trade, hailed. South Carolina: a state whose white sons did more, and did it for longer, than any other single group in the US to perpetuate slavery. Perhaps, for someone from this state, the sight of a Black man in the office of president was simply too much. It is certainly true that no one could think of any comparable incident.

It was an important reminder that, where for many of us outside the US, Obama's election was a key station on the inevitable march towards progress, to others it was an abomination that must never be repeated. The fact that in 2016 a key driver of the campaign to disavow Obama's citizenship was then elected president is an almost ludicrously literal act.

My relationship with the US has been a long and complicated one. For a start, how could I ever truly trust a people who were so uninterested in cricket?

Growing up when I did, although the US was so close – it is

only just over a hundred miles from Miami to the Bahamas –
its culture felt a long way away. The country also felt rather
vast and impenetrable. Where in the UK those from Yorkshire
like to pretend they are a distinct species from southerners,
at least a predilection for a different sort of tea and saying the
word 'bath' differently is hardly the basis for civil war. But
the US is a vast country. Montana and New York are, by most
metrics, not the same country. And the US's vastness means
that it has always looked inside first and outside second. It is
suspicious of its government in a way that I found surprising
the first few times I went there.

I was in Santa Monica. I'd just been at the White House. I
was invited to a big party in California and I thought that if I
mentioned, 'I've just been in the White House,' those present
would be very interested. But no one cared. America is an
enormous, variegated country in which truly national issues
feel so rare. You drive in your air-conditioned car, from air-
conditioned building to air-conditioned building, with your
huge cup of sugary beverage kept frigid with copious amounts
of ice. It is only when you spend time there that you see why
so much of their foreign policy has been about keeping the
cost of gasoline down. It is, in many places, an environment in
which humans cannot happily subsist without plentiful cheap
energy. Beyond that, there's a lot of issues that a lot of people
don't put in the same order. I am very mindful of Benjamin
Franklin's coining: 'A republic, if you can keep it.' One key
issue is the right to bear arms. I dislike guns. We went to
a shooting range. I never wanted to fire guns; it doesn't do
anything for me. American men couldn't understand why I
wouldn't take the chance to fire a weapon.

It is not a new thing to point out that those who confidently state that you can't change the right to bear arms enshrined in the second amendment almost never seem to remember that the second amendment is . . . an amendment. There are twenty-seven amendments to the constitution. It was almost immediately understood this was to be a live document, able to respond to unforeseen circumstances. If fifty thousand people a year dying from guns doesn't constitute a new context, I don't know what does. Secondly, if you do believe that every word is sacrosanct, its invokers almost never seem to quote the full amendment: 'A well regulated Militia, being necessary to the security of a free State, the right of the people to keep and bear Arms, shall not be infringed.' It's very specific about the context in which bearing in arms is allowable. It does not say everyone should be allowed to take a machine gun to the supermarket.

I am old enough to remember the furore in the mid-1980s that greeted the new laws to make wearing a seatbelt mandatory. There were rallies, there were cries that it was unconstitutional, unAmerican and positively communist. Freedom is an intrinsic part of the country's self-image and so any potential infringement of that is useful to a strand of their political configuration. The founding fathers knew their history. They knew how susceptible republics are to autocrats. I have no doubt that they would see the ongoing combination of Trump and the Republican Party as genuinely baffling.

I have always felt that Americans should reverse how much they care about a citizen's right to bear arms and a citizen's right to vote. I still cannot believe that election day is not a public holiday. What it means is that many – likely to be lower-wage workers – cannot go and vote during the day, and will find it harder to vote at all. This is, of course, just the latest in a long tradition of controlling who can vote, the most egregious instance of which became known as the Jim Crow laws. These involved local authorities wielding control over voter registration. As there was almost no independent observer or national standard, some voters – i.e. white voters – were simply asked their names and addresses. Black voters would be asked detailed questions about state constitutions, or given impenetrable literacy or numeracy tests. Some, like the Mississippi circuit clerk Luther Cox, became famous for asking unanswerable questions like, 'How many bubbles are in a bar of soap?' The Jim Crow laws were in action up until 1965. I note with interest that Georgia has made it illegal to bring food and water to those who are queuing to vote after work.

Since I retired from reading the news, I have been lucky enough to make documentaries. One that I think of most often was my trip to death row in the US. The US has a prison population that hovers around two million. That is about the same size as the state of Nebraska. Or, to put it another way, the prison population of the United States would comprise the second-biggest city in the UK, almost double the size of Birmingham and second only to London. And it is a prison population that is massively less white than US society – unless you hold the view that somehow something genetic makes white people more intrinsically law abiding, this imbalance of the prison population must have something to do with the way that society is organised.

I never wanted to see a prison in Britain. And I say that

as someone who had a friend in prison. And he wrote to me asking me to visit him. And, to this day, I'm ashamed of the fact I never did. I have a fear of prisons, but somehow I was persuaded to do this in America.

You had to leave your phone outside, and they would blow air through your hair to check that you weren't bringing in anything that you shouldn't bring in. Then you'd have to pass through multiple doors and guards until you got to the visitors' room. I remember laughing uproariously as an inmate told me that he'd had sex with someone who came to visit him. 'But what about all the cameras and the guards?' I asked. 'You find a way, man,' he said, smiling. 'You find a way.' He was in prison for killing a policeman, which he said was an accident. Having never been to a prison, I had assumed most inmates would deny what they were accused of. But everyone I met said they were guilty. There were often extenuating circumstances, or at least explanatory ones. The cop killer said he'd committed a burglary and was being chased by three police officers. He'd fired vaguely over his head behind them, hoping to dissuade them from following. And two of the three were dissuaded, but the third was young and keen and was hit. Shooting a police officer warranted an automatic death sentence in Indiana.

I walked past men exercising on their own in metal cages outside. I met someone called William Clyde Gibson, who'd murdered three women in cold blood. He was at great pains to tell me he'd had 'a normal childhood'. He told me he could 'kill a person then go out to dinner'. I asked him, 'Do you have any humanity?' And he sort of just shrugged and said, 'No.' The argument for the death penalty in principle is that some people commit crimes so terrible that they do not deserve to live. It is often yoked to that Old Testament concept of evil. I was stunned by what Gibson had said, and worried about what my reply would be. I told him that although I didn't believe in the death penalty, when I heard people like him express what they did in such terms, then I could understand why some people felt differently.

Another evening, we sat the cell of a person on death row. He'd killed three women. The lady who was the press officer in the prison was there as he described in fairly graphic detail what he did. She started shaking and said, 'You know, I've never heard him say that before.'

I never got it straight in my head. Some people, in an astonishing way, had reconciled themselves to what their end would be. So much so that there was one guy who, when we went back to the prison on a second visit, had been let off death row for some medical reason. And, as I talked to him, he was terribly dissatisfied about his current position: he was in this prison, not going to be killed any more on the execution table, and he said to me, 'How am I going to spend the rest of my life?' I didn't know what to say to him; whether to console him for escaping the death penalty, or not.

I spoke with one inmate, Ronald L. Sanford, and his mother, who was called Pamela. Ronald had been given a 170-year sentence at the age of fifteen for a double murder committed when he was thirteen. The crime was horrific but he should never have been sent to the prison. He would not be now.

They took me around their bright shiny new execution chamber, which was described to me as 'nice'. There were two separate viewing rooms: one for the families of the victims, and one for the families of the prisoners. But it was also fascinating to learn that many pharmaceutical companies no longer sold the required drugs to the prison as it no longer met their threshold for 'medical practice'. Though I found that positive, one can't help but worry about relying on the conscience of business to keep executions at bay. Whether or not there are some crimes for which someone 'deserves' to die I am not sure. But I know that the application of justice is not perfect: mistakes are made all the time. Had the punishment for terrorism been death, how much worse a travesty of justice would the Guildford Four case have been? And I find the public nature of executions obscene. The fact that crime makes individuals and communities angry does not mean that the state should facilitate that.

Prison policy is one of those classic issues that politics fails. Most people do not think about the treatment of prisoners. And if they do, they intuit that conditions for inmates should be poor – even though all the evidence points to societies that treat their prisoners better experiencing less crime. But in spite of this, the solution is: more jail sentencing for more crimes. Now we have private prisons for profit, which I fear is the direction of travel: more prison time for more criminals equalling more profit for private prison companies. But no political party is going to make better conditions for criminals a pillar of their manifesto.

I had dinner with my granddaughter recently and found myself arguing against her going to college in the US. I had just experienced a dose of CNN reporting on Trump's rallies, and I found myself saying to my granddaughter, 'Well, whatever you do, don't go to America.' Then I caught myself and thought, 'What are you talking about?' America is one of the most interesting and exciting countries, with so many astonishing places to go. But I fear for it. I fear for Black bodies there.

It is impossible to understand the relationship between the police and the Black community in the US if you don't remember the line you can trace back directly between the police and the 'slave patrols' who were formed to suppress uprisings and pursue and return escaped enslaved people. The whole *raison d'être* of 'slave patrols' was the capture of Black men. And you could make an argument that things haven't changed if you look at America's penal statistics. Before George Floyd there was Rodney King in 1991. Four white police officers beating a prone Black man. He was found to have been hit more than fifty times. Riots followed in 1992 when those police officers were acquitted of using excessive force by a jury.

I was making a documentary about Martin Luther King and remember talking to a US lawyer, mentioning that there were times when I was in the southern states of the US when I drove a little more quickly along the long empty stretches of road between habitation. It was those corners where I imagined that lynchings had occurred, where those ghosts might be. He looked at me with surprise. 'My friend, the lynchings occurred out front on the courthouse lawn at midday.' The last reported lynching in US was in 1981, though there are those who believe they carry on to this day but are often miscategorised as suicide.

Even today, America seems to me to be a culture driven

by such paranoia, fear and anger. And the media have a lot to answer for. The great lesson learned from the tobacco lobby was that you don't have to create a compelling counterargument. You just have to create an environment where everything is equally debased: there's no right or wrong, because you can't trust what anyone says and everyone is as bad as each other. You see it playing out again and again. The death of truth – the suspicion of professional journalism is the logical end result of that. I'm not going to pretend that the media has been perfect – certainly, the only natural human response to some of the techniques employed by the print media in the rush for a scoop is abhorrence – but this should not devalue the entire endeavour. The fundamental engine of democracy is an informed electorate, able to make decisions based on accurate information. It is only natural that there should be conflict around whether the information is the best quality it can be, and whether it is balanced.

I am grateful that I do not work as a journalist in this era of fake news, alternative facts and pervasive suspicion of the mainstream media. Things are so much quicker now. The news is a quick rush to form opinion – if you even form an opinion at all. The media seems to see its role as to display conflict as well as the process of arriving at an opinion: the constant striving for 'balance', to programme those with opposing positions as if all positions are equal, and then referee the fight. I am perhaps old fashioned and patrician for thinking that the business is to arrive at an opinion. The modern news environment leaves much less space for thought. (I am also rather glad that when I was in the public eye there was not the same panoply of dancing, ice-skating and opportunities to eat kangaroo testicles that exists in the modern world. I'm sure I would have managed to resist temptation – nobody needs to see me dance.)

There has always been a tendency in Britain to look at the US, especially its political media, and roll our eyes: 'That could never happen over here.' But we seem to be importing, wholesale, techniques from there. The spectacle of Liz Truss on Steven Bannon's show was something I could find no equivalent for in my years of reporting the news. This global network of right-wing populists sharing winning strategies is a chilling development. There is always conspiracy at its heart. And conspiracy poisons any attempt at scrutiny, this world in which we ask the question, 'Can anything ever be true'? The Downing Street parties over Covid were a case in point. At every stage we were lied to. Then those lies were denied until they couldn't be denied. I get upset because they degrade me when they say those things. What must they think of us that they treat us like such idiots? That the quality of their lying is so poor?

I have never been a lobby journalist or particularly close to UK political journalism. But it seems as if the leaping back and forth between political PR and journalism has become so close as to be one mass of friends and colleagues.

I grew up thinking that the British parliamentary system was the greatest invention in the history of civilisation. Its civility was lionised. Two members of the House who might be at each other's throats in the chamber would be able to put their differences aside and have a drink in the bar afterwards. It is so revealing that the government justification for handing out those PPE contracts to their friends was, 'We encountered an urgent problem we'd never faced before, so turned to our friends.' The idea that you do that instead of turning to experts tells you everything you need to know. The individuals involved exist in a parallel society in which personal relationships matter more than expertise. There used to be such a thing as shame. Something would happen and the call would go up: 'They've got to go.' It was understood that there were acts or events that meant you simply had to resign. That just doesn't happen any more. They stay. Hugh Dalton resigned as chancellor of the exchequer in 1947 because he had spoken to the press about the budget. Once upon a time, the budget was a serious economic thing. Now it's ideological, a party political broadcast. In the old days they would make sure to pick the provider they *didn't* know, because of the danger of it otherwise looking fishy. Perhaps it's because I am still, at heart, that boy who grew up in a small island community, who was taught to say hello, to offer directions and to attend the funerals of neighbours. That is what we did to show respect to each other. Society is, at its heart, a mutual promise we make to each other to treat each other in certain ways. And when our politicians so visibly break that promise – or act like it does not apply to them – it ripples outwards. I do not think the danger of a Boris Johnson comes from malice. He doesn't seek to hurt those around him. A precursor to malice is intent. It's more a case of: other people just don't matter. It is a repeated pattern of Johnson's life that others have reported him looking into their eyes and telling them something other than what transpires to be the truth. When I reflect upon things now, perhaps cricket and journalism are both a kind of umpire. Men like Frank Worrell and, in the same lineage, Garry Sobers were of the opinion that if you know you have touched a ball and you don't walk, even before it's called, you're a cheat. Even a moment's hesitation displayed a weakness in your character. Cricket wants to be a self-governing society, a court with no need for prosecution and defence lawyers.

When that crucible of the English public school system was producing its foot soldiers of Empire, it held the absolute need for victory in check with the gravity of fair play. If you remove that, you get figures who cheat, not through malice, but through an inability to conceive of other people as quite real enough to matter. It's not rare for politicians to look you in the eye and lie. But I'm sure that they know they are lies. The result is, consequently, a political class who are the essence of 'vaulting ambition, which o'erleaps itself. And falls on th'other'.

But this is where a political culture is so important. If you see your boss and your boss's boss commit outrageous acts and not resign, why should you? The line keeps getting moved and moved until there is no line. Inherent in the idea that a certain story breaking meant you had to resign was that it made your position untenable. As an elected official, you would be held to account. So better to fall on your sword than be set upon by the mob. But in recent years, they have not been frightened of being held to account. They hoped they could slip these things through, sneak them past.

In spite of a body of evidence to the contrary – trains, water, healthcare, energy provision – the notion that introducing market competition and a profit margin always improves things is axiomatic for some. But there are those that believe it, and believe it is the way to best raise up the most of humanity. But do I believe that this current crop believes what they say? I really don't know. It feels over recent governments as if there is a generation of politicians who are almost entirely hollow at the centre of them. Does anyone truly believe that homelessness is a 'lifestyle choice'? Or is the politics of outrage now our only mode? To cut through the torrents of noise you have to be more and more extreme, to signal that you are hard-line; to win approval in that section of the press who will give it. So much of the discussion around poverty is still built around the Victorian idea of the deserving and undeserving poor. So you tell poor people that the reason they are poor is because of the other poor people who are stealing more than their fair share.

Much of the distrust of the media and political class in Britain can be traced back to the 2003 invasion of Iraq. Looking back, it's obvious that invading Iraq caused a lot more problems than it solved. But at the time a lot of politicians on both sides of the aisle supported George W. Bush's decision to invade. They all have to live with that. However, I had met a lot of Iraqis who wanted Saddam gone too, who spoke of the legends of the torture, of the prisons; of the brutal security apparatus that ran the country. Saddam's son Uday was a sadistic psychopath. People would be kidnapped off the street by Uday's bodyguards, dragged into his limousine and never seen again. Uday also imprisoned and tortured the Iraqi Olympic football team for their poor performance.

I had one big clash with Tony Blair during the Iraq war. It was 2003 and we had assembled a studio audience, including twenty or so women who were opposed to military action.

Some of them had lost family members in September the 11th and the Bali bombing. Some said they did not want any other families to go through what they had. Some worried that the invasion would inspire further, worse terrorism. The show lasted for an hour, a real grilling. And by the end of it, Blair, clearly taken aback by the strength of the audience objections, finished rather testily with, 'You have the opportunity to reject this government at the ballot box if you don't agree with us, as is your right in a democracy.' He came out with a sheen on his forehead and snapped at Alastair Campbell as he strode past, 'Who the bloody hell's idea was that?!' And those women were proved right.

George Galloway once said that Saddam Hussein was a wonderful man. I saw George and told him in no uncertain terms I did not agree with his assessment.

A few months after Obama won his second term, I won my first as president of Surrey County Cricket Club. It was an incredible moment for me. I had been going to the Oval for more than thirty years. The first time I went, I remember someone saying that Learie Constantine had once hit a ball for six so ferociously that it had ended up in the playground of a neighbouring school. But I was never able to establish the veracity of that claim.

It pleases me that what is commonly agreed to be the first definitive recorded reference to cricket comes from a 1597 court case concerning a dispute over a plot of common land in Surrey. As part of the evidence one of the witnesses reports that they had played 'creckett' there fifty years earlier as children. Surrey and cricket go a long way back.

It has been one of the greatest constant joys of my life to sit in the Oval and watch some of the greatest players the game has ever seen – in an atmosphere unlike any other, especially when the West Indies were playing. That first day of a Test match at the Oval, walking down from the tube station, joining the crowd like a river, bright with colour, already beginning to fizz with energy ... then the ground itself, its great theatre-like quality. The iconic gasworks. Here was this place, this essential part of English cricket, which I had heard of when I was a child, listening to that battered radio. More than sixty years later they had asked me to be their president.

One afternoon, not long afterwards, at the end of a very long lunch with a group of friends, hosted by a woman I had first met in Hong Kong during the handover to China, I came to the conclusion that this lunch looked dangerously like becoming dinner, and I needed to leave. I wobbled off through Knightsbridge to get the tube home. A guy loomed over me, looked me in the eye and said, 'You don't remember me, do you?' I tried to make a joke out of it. I said I was getting on a bit and, even without the sort of lunch I'd just had, my memory sometimes failed me these days. He didn't even smile. He said, 'I was your interpreter when you interviewed Saddam Hussein.'

And I thought to myself, 'Disembowelled.'

And, Finally ...

The 2024 T20 World Cup

As I write this sentence, I am eighty-four not out, a perfectly respectable innings for most of the batsmen I have so admired. I find my thoughts turning more and more often to the things that have caused most joy in my life. And so to cricket.

We are on the eve of the T20 World Cup. It is to be jointly hosted by the West Indies and, whisper it, the US. It will feature Canada, Afghanistan, the US and Oman. By the ICC rankings, the West Indies are the fourth-best T20 team in the world, and the eighth-best Test team. These are interesting times indeed.

I have never been the sort to harrumph at cricket that is not Test cricket. Perhaps that's down to growing up on an island where cricket was, until fairly recently, only for the white man. The games I played growing up: were they conducted in the spirit of cricket? They were certainly not regulation. But they were cricket to us.

I have always believed that cricket would find its way. After all, the poet Robert Graves once described a game of cricket played in 1915 in Vermelles on the Western Front:

'The bat was a bit of rafter, the ball a rag tied with string; and the wicket a parrot cage with the clean, dry corpse of parrot inside.' He reported that play was stopped by machine-gun fire, but not before he had registered the top score – 24. That was cricket. So are the modern incarnations.

Viv Richards once said, 'One-day cricket is like fast food. No one wants to cook.' However, 50 overs now seems like a banquet, compared to Twenty20, or 10 overs, or the Hundred. I have caught the odd Hundred match and I cannot deny feeling the very real flicker of excitement when I watch an Indian Premier League match. Part of why I enjoy IPL is that it reminds me of those games I played as a child. They weren't regulation but they were my first experience of cricket. The ball is bowled, it bounces, the bat meets ball, the fielders react. The important moments are sifted out of the others. You lower the number of balls and therefore incentivise fours and sixes; you are rebalancing risk. You are minimising boredom. And that is the tenet of the modern world: successive generations encountering a world designed to obviate boredom. And cricket is part of the world. The advent of T20 and the IPL means that batters have become fitter and stronger. They are also brought up to take more risks with their shots.

During the opening ceremony of the 2023 IPL game be-tween Gujarat and Chennai, a crowd of over one hundred thousand saw a lightshow performed by fifteen hundred drones. As the lights first formed one club crest, then the other, then the IPL trophy, the crowd were frantic with ex-citement. Try telling all those people what they're watching isn't cricket. The players are in amazing physical condition;

the kind you can be when you are well compensated for your time. All is noise and colour and energy.

To watch an English county game after that is … different. It sometimes feels as if people have been predicting the death of Test cricket as long as I can remember. Of course, the simple fact is that there is as little Test cricket planned as there has ever been. Just take a look at the future tours programme. In a column in the *Guardian* in April 2023, Barney Ronay calculated that between February 2027 and mid-2031 there are six combined white-ball World Cups and five IPLs planned. Over the same period only six five-Test series are due to take place anywhere in the world.

I do have my worry about where it ultimately will lead to. Everything I've said about what I love about the game in this book may be burned away under the white heat of the attempt to make cricket a game of only sixes and fours. I sometimes worry that if every shot becomes extraordinary then perhaps none of them are?

And I do worry about those regimes who want to launder their reputations through association with certain sports – as if they can somehow have something of the cricket white rub off on themselves. The simple fact is that you cannot hold someone to account if you rely on them for your entertainment, your pleasure. If your golf and cricket and tennis are all associated with a nation state, perhaps you will feel well disposed towards them whatever they do. In 2024, it feels impossible to separate cricket from politics, if you ever could.

This was the year, after all, that Azeem Rafiq published his account of his experiences in Yorkshire cricket. The use of 'banter' as a defence felt to me to entirely miss the point.

Something being a joke has never meant that it is somehow free from the rules of society. Jokes have always been used to test the acceptable bounds of conversation. When you defend cruelty as a joke, you reduce someone to a slapstick figure whose pain is acceptable for your entertainment. But here in England, as elsewhere, there is anger at his testimony. There is a sense of constant doubling down on issues; of people talking at or past each other, mutually ascribing the worst motivation to their opponent. Every issue reaches for a kind of quick-hot moral certainty. It is not enough for your opponent to be wrong; they must be malign, evil, immoral – less than human, even. The current cultural climate feels to me to be so often defined by Macbeth's famous declaration that 'I am in blood/Stepped in so far that, should I wade no more,/ Returning were as tedious as go o'e.'

I'm aware that a call for civility can feel overly reactionary, but I cannot help but feel that an utter removal of civility makes the whole thing fall apart and result in those muddy waters that those who want apathy are desirous of. If they are all the same, then nothing will change. It is a corruption of democracy. The enemy of change is apathy, and apathy comes from a feeling that things can never change.

I saw in Northern Ireland how sectarianism is driven by a focus on the most recent violation. 'We did that to you because you did that to us.' 'But we did that to you because you did that to us.' And so on and so on, back through time. I saw how apartheid progressed by its banality. The violence does not resolve. It echoes down the generations as the children who experience it are twisted by their exposure to it. I always struggled to keep my emotions in check when I reported on stories where children had been impacted. There were famines and droughts where women could no longer produce milk to feed their children. In South Africa these were the direct results of a policy that valued one group of people less than the others.

I find I cannot physically look at some of the images from Gaza. And this is without journalists allowed there. What we have seen has been conveyed without any real reporting. That violence, on 7 October, and the days, weeks and months after it will not dissipate for generations. I proffer no easy summation of a deeply complicated and horrific situation. But I continue to believe that the driving principle behind situations like this should be minimising the number of children that encounter violence. I refuse to believe that violence is justified and will never agree with those who subscribe to the omelette chef model of history. Although it is in many ways a human impulse to compare, to catalogue, to set in some sort of hierarchy, with war and other humanitarian situations that seems to me to be grotesque. The idea that you cannot express an opinion on one conflict unless you've been vocal on another; the fact that 'worse things' have happened means that this horror is lessened – the answer seems, to me, that we should express horror at more of the world's events, not fewer.

No, we cannot ignore the past. It is a simple fact that those so often asking whether we can't move forwards from the past are those whose ancestors benefited from it. Of course, you cannot hold people accountable now for the events of the past as individuals. But to try to say to someone that the fact my great-great-grandfather may have owned shares in yours has no bearing on life now seems ludicrous to me. If you begin a relay race with one team 100 metres ahead, it's not hard to predict what will happen. The fact that it might make some people feel guilty or bad to admit this fact seems to me to be a price worth paying. When you have grown up watching your father work his heart out and not be rewarded as he should, you learn that sometimes the cards you are dealt decide the game.

The colonial experiment, a concatenation of historical accidents, one after the other, was processed as manifest destiny. When religion was the dominant lens, the Africans were soulless heathens who could not be trusted with their own salvation. When evolution became part of the conversation, they were a less evolved version of humanity. The new science of genetics was co-opted so that humans could be divided and ranked with white at the top and Black at the bottom. For three hundred years this particularly virulent expression of slavery marshalled all of the available tools to justify itself. This was the era of dividing up the maps of the world. The Berlin Conference. The Radcliffe Line. The Sykes–Picot Agreement. The straight lines driven through millions of people's lives. Then the horror when violence erupts. How 'uncivilised'. We still live in a world defined by the fragmentation of imposed identities. Everywhere you look, you see the legacy of that mindset, of chopping up and slicing the map, maintaining European interests thousands of miles away. As someone who grew up in a colony, I have some small insight into what it feels like from the inside. I was twenty-four years old when Trinidad achieved independence, part of the sequence of dominoes that fell after the Second World War, beginning with the partition of India, the Suez crisis and on through the independence of colonies.

We must, of course, be careful not to project our mores backwards in time. Individuals cannot be held solely accountable for attitudes of the time. But we must also make sure that is not a blank cheque. There we some who delighted in colonialism's hierarchies more than others.

That cherished fantasy of 'taking back control' is actually a fantasy of retreating from the world as it is now – into some dimly remembered past, if it ever existed at all. We need immigrants for the United Kingdom to function properly. That is a fact. This idea that we can pull the drawbridge up and this will lead to Britain somehow regaining global centrality is a fantasy. Those days are long gone. I saw an interview with a senior Chinese official who listened politely as the interviewer spoke of the rivalry between China and Britain then smiled and said that Britain must learn to live with China, not as a rival, but as a fact of life.

There is much made of those new to this country needing to buy into British values. But for that to hold firm it must be clear what those are. They must be admirable values. When our political class debase those values, they blame it all on the vulnerable who come to these shores seeking safety. I cannot condone that.

In times of inequality, the demagogues and popularists come out to make hay. They blame immigrants. They blame the enemies within. They accuse the press of betraying the nation. There is no criticism of them that cannot be absorbed into their paranoid fantasy. You can get ahead in the Conservative and Republican parties by being a Black or brown person willing to front the sharp end of right-wing politics. This is not to say that you can't be a person from that background with those beliefs. Just that it is an observable fact that you are useful, and that utility has a value.

I read an article by Dominic Cummings, claiming that Brexit represented, among many other things, the successful division of home owners and home renters. And that feels to me to be a more useful dividing line than simple age. The gap between those two groups feels like it may come to be the realisation of H. G. Wells's famous Morlocks and Eloi. I grew up in a tiny island community. I know how resentments and jealousies fester, how protective people can be about the ecosystem of their own culture. But I also know that the solution is respect, politeness and kindness. Treating others as you would want to be treated yourself is the essence of how humans find common cause. I think of my mother and how it is better to treat strangers as if they are angels.

The idea of the island race fearful of 'invasion' has always been a part of the English self-image. History teaches us that blaming those who are the most recent additions to a society will always find approval with a section of the populace. Whether it is those people in the small boats now, or the Polish, Somalians, Indians, Pakistanis, Caribbeans, Jews, Irish or Huguenots before them, there will always be someone you can blame the ills of society on. These demagogues come with a smile, with a brusque charm forged in business, with an appeal to common sense over a pint in the pub. I came to Britain a year after Enoch Powell made his infamous 'Rivers of Blood' speech. What a certain sort of politician does now is not new. They do it because human beings must be encouraged towards common cause. It is difficult. It involves compromise, it involves competition. Humans want to feel a sense of belonging, and often the engine of belonging is fuelled by excluding those who we are not like; the point is to manufacture a sense of identity, not through shared values but through weaponised fear, through a constant aggression against what we are not.

I was sat next to Theresa May once at the cricket during her premiership. The chairman of Surrey called me up and requested I sit next to her. I thought it best to steer clear of any really political topics, but the Labour Party conference was on, and I observed that none of the people in the crowd at the Oval would hear Corbyn's words. She said absolutely nothing. Perhaps she felt uneasy in case our conversation turned inexorably towards Windrush and the 'hostile environment' policy. I hated the 'hostile environment' policy. I was horrified by the 'hostile environment' as an idea. What chilling language. What blunt force to apply to people's lives. We now know how many of the Windrush generation were caught up in it. And what a shame that hangs perpetually over those who designed and implemented its policies.

No country can have utterly open borders, unless all do. But borders must be enforced without hate in an environment that does not rely on the slow degradation of us all. It seems to me to be a simple matter of humanity to treat those applying for asylum as if they are fully deserving of it until the moment it is certain they are not. It should not be the other way around. To design a system that operates under the assumption you are a liar until the moment you are not, is to fail the lowest basic threshold of civilisation. Perhaps this is yet again due to my upbringing, to parents who believe that you should welcome everyone to your table. That you should greet everyone with respect. The manufactured hate for immigrants through political expediency is an act of utter cowardice. The demagogues who profit from it are poisoning the well of society. It will never not work to blame everything on the other, to whip up hatred. But it will never suddenly become right. It is the small politics of division.

Those who decry immigration often make it sound a casual choice. But to leave your home is no easy thing. As the Somali British poet Warsan Shire put it so beautifully, you only leave your home if it is 'the mouth of a shark'.[15]

I sometimes feel slightly depressed when I read in the news that we're sending a probe up to Mars. If our ultimate hope is to colonise it, what are the chances that within a generation there will be war between the Mars population and us? We have been able to find axioms of difference that split the two ends of the same street apart, so what hope is there that we won't carry the seeds of division up there?

What soothes my mind is the thought of the first Mars against Earth Test match, played with a white ball so as to be visible against the red soil.

In writing this book I have left out an awful lot. There are hundreds if not thousands of hours of watching cricket that didn't make the cut. I certainly don't want to give the impression I have only watched the West Indian national team play. I have enjoyed watching a great deal of cricket from very many places. I've watched games in India, Australia and South Africa.

I saw the great Peter May play a memorable over against a Trinidadian bowler when he shouldered his bat, not playing a shot. There was something about the way he did it that I will never forget. I remember sitting and watching on one memorable occasion in August 1994 when Devon Malcolm, in response to a bouncer that struck him while at bat, took 9 for 57 in one of the single finest pieces of fast bowling there has ever been. I covered the cricket in Sydney in 1979 when Roger Tolchard, the English wicketkeeper, was hit in the face from a ball from Dennis Lillee and had a fractured cheek, which ruled him out for the rest of the series. So, the weekend before he was due to fly home, before I followed the team on to their next match, we drank Houghton's White Burgundy and ate barramundi and chips looking out over Sydney Harbour, as the light glinted off hundreds of tiny boats; the Sydney Harbour Bridge in one direction, the opera house in the other. I remember thinking what a fine thing indeed life was. I said, 'Roger, I think we've died and gone to heaven.'

I've left out almost the entirety of my emotional life outside of cricket. This is because those are my family's and others' stories to tell, not because they have not been my life's great joy.

There is nothing finer than being allowed to be a parent. To be responsible in some way for forming a child's view of the universe; to help develop and shape the emergence of a young life. It is the great honour of my life.

I watched my son get married recently. The wedding was organised by his friends. To see his friendships, the love for him, was a source of great happiness. To have a family. To watch your children grow. To communicate to them that they are safe and loved. To see them go out into the world and meet people, form friendships and fall in love. What a gift. The greatest sadness is that for all of us there will come a time when we no longer see that for ourselves. But to know it will continue is a source of great comfort. I understand why people may not want to have children. Of course. But I will never understand those who are proud that they find children boring. Children are people. If you find children boring, you find people boring. And if you find people boring, my friend, the problem may, in fact, be you.

The finest thing in humanity is the common purpose that binds us. Selfishness, whether of community or gene, seems these days to be a defining characteristic. So we must embrace those moments when it is put aside, when we are drawn together in commonality and purpose – and games are something that do that – they bring us together. I admire individual sports. But I love team sports. Because it is when human beings are united in common purpose that we are at our finest. A cricket match when it is played in the right spirit is one organism. There are two teams, two sets of players seeking to win, but they become one thing. As a child and as a man I have always been someone who followed the rules. There is, of course, a seriousness to following rules passed down when you are a colonised people. The stakes are very high. But there is also a kind of joy in following the rules of cricket: because to win playing the right way feels even sweeter. And in cricket everyone is under the same edicts. To follow the rules when others don't have to is a chore. We know that people cheat, they commit crime, when they feel

that the world isn't set up for them. What's the point of following the rules if the game is stacked against you? Does it
make you a sucker to take colonialism at its word? To follow
the rules? To believe that if you play up you will succeed? I
prefer to think of it as a kind of faith. One that both of my
parents passed on to me. It is an act of faith to believe that
others will behave well. It is this great experiment called
society. It is one I am grateful for when I witness the orderly
transfer of power in Britain, when compared to the United
States.

You can't separate how you feel about new things from
your age. You have a sense of yourself as a certain sort of
person. Part of getting older is finding new ideas harder to get
your head around. But I am lucky enough to still travel about,
to play the odd game of tennis. But I do worry for my children
and their children and their children's children. There are a
great many things that seem so much harder now. But then
I'm sure I was told that by 'old' people when I was a child
and confidently discounted it. I recently saw where Constable
painted *The Hay Wain* when I went for a walk in Dedham
Vale. I first encountered the painting in a book, growing up in
Trinidad. Did it mean less to me because I had not set foot in
a landscape such as that when I first saw it? Who can say? All
I know is that I remember feeling something when I looked
at that painting as a child.

One thing that has always held true of my life is that
there are always good people. I may have been in a country
because of terrible events. But there were always good, generous, kind people struggling to be happy. I would arrive in
a country and start to talk to the taxi driver, and that would

be the beginning of trying to find out what was going on, of thinking about how to tell the story so that someone might understand it, as I did listening to the person telling it to me face to face. People put themselves out, put themselves in danger, for no other reason than that someone else was in need. I was once struggling to get our videos out from Beirut during the conflict. I did it a couple of times myself, but it was a terrifying, fraught experience and I was desperate not to do it again. And our concierge suggested I try offering a hundred dollars to a taxi driver to take them to Damascus. And then, as I sat waiting for the confirmation from London that my material had got to Damascus, I suddenly thought, 'I didn't take the number of this taxi, I didn't ask him his name.' And yet I would sit in the bar and wait for a call, and it would eventually come, and somebody in London would say, 'We can see your pictures.' And I thought, 'What a wonderful man to have done that.' My overriding memory is of the goodness of people.

It was what made Nelson Mandela the extraordinary man that he was – his ability to keep that in mind when all of the available evidence might have swayed his certainty. If you are able to begin by looking for the good in people, the first principle that you will treat each other well, rather than the inverse, I do not believe you will go far wrong in life.

I was born on a small island. I have spent the rest of my life on another. Cricket is the line strung between the two. We find others. We agree on the rules. We play. Cricket, like life, only means anything because of other people.

Notes

1. Arlott, John and Eagar, Patrick (1979), *An Eye for Cricket* (London: Hodder and Stoughton).
2. Cardus, Neville (1930), *Cricket* (London: Longmans, Green)
3. Reuters New Delhi, 'Mike Brearley: The man with a "degree in people"', *Gulf Times*, 28 April 2020, https://www.gulf-times.com/story/661861/mike-brearley-the-man-with-a-degree-in-people.
4. Kimber, Jarrod, 'Worrell, Weekes and Walcott: One pair of hands, three greats, three Ws', *Cricketer*, 2 July 2020, https://www.thecricketer.com/Topics/features/everton_weekes_west_indies_clyde_walcott_frank_worrell_jarrod_kimber_west_indies_cricket.html.
5. Ibid.
6. James, C. L. R. (1963), *Beyond a Boundary* (London: Hutchinson)
7. Ibid.
8. Preston, Norman (ed.) (1962), *Wisden Almanac* (London: Sporting Handbooks), https://www.espncricinfo.com/wisdenalmanack/content/story/155246.html.
9. James, C. L. R. (1963), *Beyond a Boundary* (London: Hutchinson).
10. Burnton, Simon (2020), 'Garry Sobers and the risky declaration that enlivened a dour series', *Guardian*, 17 March, https://www.theguardian.com/sport/blog/2020/mar/17/garry-sobers-and-the-risky-declaration-that-enlivened-a-dour-series-the-spin-cricket.
11. McDonald, Trevor (1984), *Viv Richards: The Authorized Biography* (London: Pelham).
12. Day, Meagan (2021), 'How cricket became a symbol of West Indian pride', *Tribune*, 26 June, https://tribunemag.co.uk/2021/06/how-cricket-became-a-symbol-of-west-indian-pride.
13. Lister, Simon (2020), 'How Clive Lloyd's West Indies restored joy and respect to the Caribbean diaspora', *Wisden*, 2 November, https://www.wisden.com/cricket-features/how-clive-lloyds-west-indies-restored-joy-and-respect-to-the-caribbean-diaspora.
14. Hoult, Nick (2021), 'The greatest over ever bowled: Sir Geoffrey Boycott and Michael Holding remember the six balls that shook the world', *Telegraph*, 11 March, https://www.telegraph.co.uk/cricket/

2021/03/11/greatest-over-geoffrey-boycott-michael-holding-balls-
shook-world/.
15. Shire, Warsan (2022), 'Home', in *Bless the Daughter Raised by a Voice Inside Her Head* (London: Chatto & Windus).

Acknowledgements

This book would have been impossible without the assistance of numerous club officials and a wide variety of international sportsmen. I am particularly indebted to scores of West Indian cricketers who gave me so much of their time long before I came to Britain. I was fortunate to have so many conversations with Frank Worrell, Clive Walcott, Garry Sobers, Wes Hall, Gordon Greenidge and many others. Much later I was fortunate to be asked to write personal portraits of Viv Richards and Clive Lloyd. In Britain I travelled the world to report on cricket matches and to meet players of every Test match playing country. I retain vivid memories of conversations with former England Captain Mike Brearley and Australian legend Richie Benaud. As a member of the Surrey Cricket Club, where I was once president, I have been in constant contact with players and club officials who could not have been more open in sharing with me their philosophy of the great game. The managers of the Surrey Cricket Club could not have been more helpful.

Thanks to my Publisher Sharmaine Lovegrove and her brilliant team at Dialogue, Jamie Coleman and my literary agent, Robert Caskie, for finding and bringing this project to me. Finally, I am indebted to my agent, Anita Land, who patiently supervised communication with the publishers during the creation of this book.

Bringing a book from manuscript to what you are reading is a team effort.

Renegade Books would like to thank everyone who helped to publish *On Cricket* in the UK.

Editorial
Sharmaine Lovegrove
Eleanor Gaffney

Contracts
Anniina Vuori
Imogen Plouviez
Amy Patrick
Jemima Coley

Sales
Caitriona Row
Dominic Smith
Frances Doyle
Ginny Mašinović
Rachael Jones
Georgina Cutler
Toluwalope Ayo-Ajala

Design
Nico Taylor

Production
Narges Nojoumi

Publicity
Millie Seaward

Marketing
Emily Moran
Mia Oakley

Operations
Kellie Barnfield
Millie Gibson
Sameera Patel
Sanjeev Braich

Finance
Andrew Smith
Ellie Barry

Audio
Dominic Gribben

Copy-Editor
Ian Preece

Proofreader
David Bamford